Squeak—A Quick Trip to ObjectLand

Gene Korienek

Tom Wrensch

Doug Dechow

Addison-Wesley

Boston • San Francisco • New York • Toronto • Montreal
London • Munich • Paris • Madrid
Capetown • Sydney • Tokyo • Singapore • Mexico City

The publisher offers discounts on this book when ordered in quantity for special sales. For more information, please contact:

Pearson Education Corporate Sales Division
201 W. 103rd Street
Indianapolis, IN 46290
(800) 428-5331
corpsales@pearsoned.com

Visit AW on the Web: www.aw.com/cseng/

Library of Congress Cataloging-in-Publication Data

Korienek, Gene.
Squeak—a quick trip to ObjectLand / Gene Korienek, Tom Wrensch, Doug Dechow.—[Updated ed.]
p. cm.
Updated ed. of: A quick trip to ObjectLand. c1993.
Includes bibliographical references and index.
ISBN 0-201-73114-2 (pbk.)
1. Object-oriented programming (Computer science) 2. Smalltalk (Computer program language) 3. Squeak. I. Wrensch, Tom. II. Dechow, Doug. III. Korienek, Gene. Quick trip to ObjectLand. IV. Title.

QA76.64 .K66 2002
005.13'3 2001053542

ISBN: 0-201-73114-2
Text printed on recycled paper

1 2 3 4 5 6 7 8 9 10—MA—0504030201

First printing, December 2001

We dedicate this rather funny, hopefully interesting, complete, accurate, compilable, and educational work to ourselves, because we actually finished this tome.

```
(Earth allLifeForms humans)
    select: [:being |
        #('Gene Korienek' 'Tom Wrensch' 'Doug Dechow')
            includes: being name]
```

We also dedicate this book to Blacky the dog, who contributed large quantities of drool and tail wagging to the last version of this book and who, unfortunately, is no longer instantiated.

```
(Earth allLifeForms canines labrador retrievers)
    select: [:being | being name = 'Blacky']
```

Contents

Preface

We have read our share of programming-language books and have learned much and little. The style used by conventional programming-language books is a blend between that of a reference book and that of a code-examples book, with some explanatory comments squeezed in between. When approaching the creation of this book, we never considered writing it in a conventional format. The unconventional nature of Smalltalk demands a novel approach. So, we wrote the book in the form of dialogues involving a human named Jim, who has reasons to converse about the nuances of the object-oriented paradigm, Smalltalk programming, and the Squeak environment. The dialogues take place between Jim and the Objective Wizard (an outspoken, outlandish, and outstanding object) in some chapters, and between Jim and the Objective Librarian (a well-spoken and reflective object) in other chapters.

It bears noting that the setting for this book is the virtual world of ObjectLand. However, since, as of yet, humans are unable to enter ObjectLand, you will want to keep in mind that ObjectLand's real-world analogue is Squeak.

The intent of this book is to teach the reader to solve problems in the object-oriented paradigm and to implement solutions using the object-oriented programming language called Smalltalk in the Squeak environment. It must be read from start to finish and read completely. As you read it, you will soon realize that it is not a reference book. It is more like a storybook with To Do Lists. Read it as you would read a story. It has a plot; it has character; it's meant to entertain.

The other big difference between this book and conventional programming books is that you should have a current version of Squeak running in a computer next to you while you are reading. You can participate in the story, and the To Do Lists ask you to complete tasks to reinforce the chapters' information.

The conversation between Jim and the Objective Wizard contains English sentences interspersed with Smalltalk code. You can easily recognize the Smalltalk code because it is always in a different typeface—`this one`.

This book can be read in about 15 sittings. That's one chapter per sitting. The completion of the To Do Lists is mandatory. A To Do List appears at the conclusion of each chapter. You will notice that the completed To Do code is not included with the book. The reason for this is that we all know you will look at it as soon as a To Do task gets difficult. We don't want you to look at our solutions to these tasks. We want you to work through the difficulties and reap the learning rewards. If you really want to see our solutions, then check the "About the Authors" section to find out where we are.

Learning Smalltalk and the Squeak environment can be a tricky task, but after teaching introductory and advanced Smalltalk classes for a few years, we have figured out how people learn to use Smalltalk. We have found this book's approach to be an extremely effective path to understanding the object-oriented concepts and gaining skill in solving problems by writing squeaky clean code—in Squeak.

Try it, it works!

Once you have completed this book, you probably will not need it again. You will have been introduced to the cast of characters and will have learned the story. You will need a more advanced book. We suggest that you continue your journey up the Smalltalk learning curve by rambling through the list of texts for further reading that we've included in the back of this book—or perhaps, look for a future ObjectLand book someday.

Gene Korienek
Tom Wrensch
Doug Dechow
August 2001

Acknowledgments

Dr. Gene Korienek has come to know not only that "no person is an island" but also that "no person gets anything done alone." It seems that anything worth doing requires a team: Tom Wrensch and Doug Dechow allowed Gene to coerce them into coauthoring this book. There are none better than these two.

We all exist in systems of one kind or another. An important member of Gene's local socio-system—Deanne Hudson, his highly significant other, and very supportive and cute female human—was instrumental in the completion of this book. In addition, Gene acknowledges the members of his local ecosystem: Lucky, Bucky, Vega, Jupiter, Elvis, and a cast of thousands.

In the first, and now highly collectible, version of this book, Gene acknowledged a number of friends who had had an impact on his thinking over the years. He mentions them again here for those of you who failed to read the classic version: Guy Asbury, Bill Bazan, Craig Brigham, Larry Brown, Mario DeSario, and Lynne Griffin.

Dr. Tom Wrensch wishes to acknowledge the contributions made to this project by Beverly Wrensch and Eric Scharff. Eric was particularly helpful with suggestions and questions about Squeak. Beverly's name is on the list so that Tom doesn't get in trouble.

Doug Dechow thoroughly enjoyed the opportunity to coauthor this updated version of Gene and Tom's classic Smalltalk text. On several occasions, David Dechow was able to answer questions and produce materials in a turnaround time that bordered on instantaneous; David's older, better-looking brother really appreciated it. Finally, Anna Leahy provided support, encouragement, and feedback at every step of the project.

All of the authors are grateful for the cooperation and contributions of the three editors at Addison-Wesley who saw this project through: Mike Hendrickson, Heather Olszyk, and Ross Venables. Thanks are also due the members of the Addison-Wesley production staff. Also, as this project was coming down the homestretch, Dr. Anna Leahy of Missouri Western State College pulled it all together. She served as a de facto preproduction editor for the book; her assistance in formatting, editing, and tidying saved the authors from having to do these tasks.

About the Authors

The authors reside in ObjectLand and can be contacted only by specific message sends. They have taken up residence in ObjectLand because life is encapsulated there and because it is okay to respond with `doesNotUnderstand`.

Gene Korienek lives in the northwestern quadrant of ObjectLand. Being self-employed, he is doing whatever he wants to do. At the moment, Gene spends his time hiking, fishing, sailing, and starting up a robotics company. More information about Gene can be found at *http://www.3sigmarobotics.com/staff/korienek.html.*

Tom Wrensch currently lives in Western ObjectLand. He can be contacted electronically at *twrensch@acm.org*. Other forms of communication tend to bounce. Tom lives with two humans, two cats, and four computers. This mismatch of five animate beings and four computers works well only because one of the cats is a Luddite.

When not writing, designing software, or implementing strange new programs, Tom has been known to eat and sleep. He is currently a subclass of `Professor` with the value of `'computer science'` in the instance variable `department`. He still really hates getting up early.

Doug Dechow can be located in the Pacific-Northwestern portion of ObjectLand. Doug is instantiated from a subclass of `Student`—`GraduateStudent`—in the Computer Science Department at Oregon State University. The class-subclass relationship described in the preceding sentence contains more irony than the creators of Smalltalk probably intended.

Currently, most of Doug's efforts are focused on research in the area of programming languages. In his copious free time, he occasionally writes books and consults for his brothers Richard and David and his pseudobrother Donovan at Dechow Consulting. His sisters—Emily and Suellen—wisely chose other career paths.

Part I

Welcome to ObjectLand

0

As Our Story Begins

Jim, a member of a software development group for a Fortune 100 corporation, joins two colleagues in the corporate coffee room. He loosens his tie, then rubs his eyes. His friends are discussing the difficulties inherent to their jobs: the high cost of developing software; how difficult it is to change; and that it doesn't work quite right and is often error prone, in spite of the substantial time invested in its creation.

Jim nods sympathetically. He knows just what they mean. He's been puzzling through a development problem for days. Overwhelmed, he feels himself slumping into his chair, his hand around his coffee mug.

"Hey, fellas! Couldn't help but overhear!" A new member of the development team leans across from a neighboring table. "But don't despair. It's a simple matter—all you need to know about are objects, messages, methods, inheritance, polymorphism, and encapsulation." The man stands, fishes in his jeans pocket, and pulls out a brochure. He flips it to Jim and wiggles his eyebrows. "Just came back from there myself. Might be the answer to your problems."

Jim picks up the brochure as the new employee walks toward the door. Just before leaving the room, the man stops and turns. "You'll see, fellas. The design process can be more intuitive! Complexity can be managed!" Then, the fellow employee disappears into the corridor.

Jim looks at the brochure. It reminds him of a brochure his mother sent him once—something about a cruise. Jim remembers he lost seven vacation days that year because he didn't use them. Too many projects, too many errors, too many…

"Objects? Inheritance?" one of Jim's friends asks. "Do you know what that guy was talking about?"

Jim shrugs his shoulders as the other team members say good-bye and leave him alone to page through the brochure. The pamphlet recommends a revitalizing seminar for students and developers of software—at a place called ObjectLand. There, participants can enjoy high rates of code reuse through the design of general forms of specific solutions. The brochure boasts that guests can bask in the warmth of specialized forms of the solutions benefiting from something called "inheritance."

As Jim reads, his vision blurs. Exhausted from long hours at his desk, he closes his eyes. "Boy, I'm tired," he thinks. "I sure could use a new perspective." Jim's world begins to spin—from his third cup of coffee this morning, he thinks—and slowly his chin sinks to his chest, the brochure still in his hand. But immediately he awakens...

or so he believes...

JIM	OBJECTIVE WIZARD

JIM: Hmgph, hmm, hey, where am I?

OBJECTIVE WIZARD:

```
ObjectLand location: Jim.
```

JIM: Good morning?

OBJECTIVE WIZARD:

```
PopUpMenu inform:
  ((Time now
     between: (Time new hours: 0
                          minutes: 0
                          seconds: 0)
     and: (Time new hours: 12
                  minutes: 0
                  seconds: 0))
ifFalse: ['Not morning']
ifTrue:  ['Good morning']).
```

JIM: What did you say?

JIM: And where's my coffee?

OBJECTIVE WIZARD: Oh, excuse me. I mistook you to be a resident of ObjectLand. Clearly, you are a visitor. I see from your label that you are named Jim—a human, no less. I am called the Objective Wizard.

You were probably sending me a morning greeting. That is rote behavior for most humans. In ObjectLand—in what you, in the real world, know as the Squeak environment—we do that sort of thing by sending the morning message to the greeting object. The expression looks like the following:

```
Greeting morning.
```

JIM: What the heck are you talking about?

OBJECTIVE WIZARD: The value returned from this message send is determined by the greeting object, but a return is always guaranteed.

Why have you come to ObjectLand?

JIM: Who knows? I read some brochure.

JIM	OBJECTIVE WIZARD
	Very well. Are there concepts about which you would like to know?
Well, while I'm actually here, I wouldn't mind hearing something about objects and messages and such.	
	In spite of your confusion, you have come to the right place, Jim. Everything here in ObjectLand is an object. We objects can respond only to messages sent to us, and our methods determine our responses. If you wish to communicate with me and with the other objects in ObjectLand, you must know that each of us has our own set of methods, one method for each message to which we know how to respond. Sometimes we inherit these methods from our "parents," and sometimes they are part of our own definitions. So, if you are interested in objects, you are looking at one. Send me any message you want, and I will execute one of my methods and return an object to you.
Excuse me, but there must be some misunderstanding. I am from a software development group in an important company, and I need to learn about software objects, messages, and methods. What can you tell me about them?	
	Jim, you must understand that ObjectLand is not real. It is a virtual place. You are here in mind only, and only because you have an interest in taking to heart, as humans say, the object-oriented paradigm. All objects with which you communicate here will be virtual—that is, software—objects. I am what you would call a software object, and, for all I know—and I do know virtually (Smalltalk joke) all—you may be one also.
Please, no metaphysics. Just software.	

JIM

OBJECTIVE WIZARD

You see, Jim, objects view the world through the messages sent to them. All I really know about you is that you are an object sending me messages. Any message you send to me activates a method that I have inside me. You are now listening to my response to your last message.

And it's a long one.

The verbosity of my response is related to the message you sent; you have requested information of a complex nature. Let us go on.

As you know, objects exist in the physical world. You are very familiar with them. Your watch, for example, is a physical-world object. Objects can also exist in your design world. If your programming language supports objects, then you can extend the existence of your objects from the design world into your implementation world. Here in Object-Land—in our ever-so-lovely Squeak environment—the programming language of choice is Smalltalk. I happen to be an object implemented in Smalltalk.

Objects in Smalltalk are containers of information (variables), behavior (methods), and messages to activate the methods. In Smalltalk, individual objects are not defined explicitly. Instead, you define classes of objects, and the individual objects are instances of the classes that characterize them.

Wait a minute, this sounds important. You seem to be describing objects by using the terms *object*, *message*, and *method*. I just want to understand what an object is.

Please don't confuse me.

Humans can be easily confused, particularly when faced with new concepts, which humans try to relate to their preexisting notions.

Jim, the word *object* refers to a conceptual entity that contains both state and behavior or, in more conventional terms,

Jim	Objective Wizard
	variables and code that can get and set the values of those variables.
	Another way of thinking about an object is to consider it as a package of information and descriptions of the manipulations of that information.
	Jim, you can be thought of as an object. I can say this because I know you contain some information or variables (that is, name, age, address, and so on). I also know you can exhibit behavior. I have observed you behave. If I sent you the `name` message, you would behave by answering your name.
Are you saying I'm predictable?	
	No, but when thinking in object-oriented terms, you could be the receiving object of a message called "name." When you received the `name` message, you executed a chunk of code called a "method"—in this case, your name method, which results in your behavior (that is, verbalizing your name).
Hey, this almost makes sense!	
	Of course it does. You are learning quickly. I accept you as my student. Congratulations.
Wait a minute! I'm very busy. I have a job, a girlfriend, and a lot going on. How long will it take to learn enough to create some objects and take them back to my company?	
	Well, if you are willing to spend several hours a day, in a week you will be ready to begin implementing objects.
You mean it takes only a week to learn to program in Squeak?	
	No, it takes only a week or two to learn the object-oriented concepts, Smalltalk syntax, and Squeak programming environment. You will also learn how to learn Smalltalk. This last bit of knowledge will be the most valuable, for it will carry you the rest of the way to your goal.

JIM	OBJECTIVE WIZARD
Teach the students to teach themselves, so to speak.	
	Do you wish to be my student? Do you wish to learn something now—to be all you can be, and escape the spaghetti-code world?
Yes, I suppose it's about time I did something about my frustrations with programming. You know, take responsibility and see if I can find a better way to approach things.	
	Have you been viewing the Oprah object?
	So, you are willing to spend some time in ObjectLand?
Yes. How do I start?	
	Send the `turn` message to the `page` object.
Okay, will this compile? `(Page now) turn`	
	Well done, Jim.

1

A View of ObjectLand

Contents at: 'Chapter 1'

#(

installation
   necessary files
   tools

platforms

start-up screen
   Welcome to...
   The Worlds of Squeak

navigating
   the mouse
   World menu

exiting the environment
   save
   save as...
   save and quit
   quit

Morphic project
   flaps and tabs

first tools
   Workspace
   Transcript).

Questions of Interest

- Which platforms does Squeak run on?
- How do I access a World menu?
- How do I start and stop Squeak?
- How do I save the current state of my work?
- Where can I find more Smalltalk information?
- How does Squeak work with my mouse?
- How do I open a new Morphic project?
- How do I navigate between Morphic projects?
- What is the Workspace?
- What is the Transcript?

Introduction

Hello again. Today, you are going to take a field trip into the ObjectLand library.

In this chapter, you will learn to install and begin using the Squeak environment on your own computer. While some concepts and menus might seem familiar at first glance, be sure to keep an open mind as you learn how to use Squeak. As a trip into the library, this chapter also provides numerous references to which you can refer back as needed.

By the end of this chapter, you will understand a little about two important tools: the Workspace and the Transcript. These tools will continue to be important in allowing you to prototype new applications and tools as you progress in your understanding and use of the Squeak environment.

Goals for This Chapter

- To understand how to install the Squeak environment on your computer.
- To learn how to use the mouse in the Squeak environment.
- To learn the following commands in a Morphic project by using the following menu commands:

Open	Quit
Save	Naming
Save as	Print it
Save and Quit	

- To use the Workspace and the Transcript to execute and observe the results of very basic code.

Jim	Objective Librarian
Hey, this is different! Where am I now?	
	Greetings, Jim! If you remember from your initial encounter with the Objective Wizard, you can find your location by sending the following message: `ObjectLand location: Jim.` You have been transported to the ObjectLand library. I'm the Objective Librarian. I'm an instance of the librarian object. The following message send `self name` reveals that my name is Objective Librarian. I'm friendly and helpful, and I'm going to take you on a tour of the Squeak environment.
Nice to meet you, Objective Librarian. You're a welcome relief. But why am I here?	
	The aim of this tour is for you to become familiar with your surroundings in ObjectLand. Since you're a new visitor to ObjectLand, this tour will guide you through the basics. If you feel that the tour is too basic for your needs, by all means, feel free to wander around on your own. Whatever your level of experience, we hope that you find your stay here in the library a pleasant one. Let's begin by making sure that you have the proper environment present on the laptop that I see you've brought.
Can I get an espresso first?	
	Sure, Jim. In fact, I'm thinking you could use a double. But make it quick. We need to begin.
Okay. I'm set. How do I make sure I can use Squeak on my laptop?	
	If you don't already have a copy of Squeak installed on your computer, you need to install one now.

JIM	OBJECTIVE LIBRARIAN
I don't have it installed. Can you tell me how to do that?	
	Do you have an Internet connection?
Yes.	
	Good. The easiest way to install the most recent version of Squeak is to point your Web browser at *http://www.squeak.org* and follow the downloading instructions. A copy of Squeak is also available on the book's CD.
What should I do now that the latest version is downloaded to my own computer?	
	Just use the tools appropriate to your system to unpack the download; you will be left with a directory or folder full of the files necessary to run Squeak. At a minimum, there are probably four files: SqueakV3.sources Squeak3.x.changes Squeak3.x.image Virtual Machine executable Although the names of files are somewhat platform dependent and vary between versions of Squeak, you can figure out which file is which.
My office uses Windows, Unix, and Macintosh. Could you tell me more about using Squeak on the different platforms so I'll have some basic info regardless of my platform?	
	On both Windows and Unix machines (Linux, Solaris, and so on), you will need to create a directory to hold the unpacked files. For Unix machines, the natural choice is to use the GNU tools—gzip and tar. The following command entered at the

JIM | OBJECTIVE LIBRARIAN

shell prompt will successfully uncompress and extract the virtual machine:

```
gunzip file-name.tar.gz | tar xvf –
```

For Windows, we recommend using WinZip. When using WinZip, you can create a directory to hold the Squeak distribution via the **Extract** screen. Some people find it easier to create a new directory by using a GUI rather than the command line.

If Stuffit Expander is installed on your Macintosh, it automatically unpacks the download. In Expander's preferences, make sure that you have the "Cross Platform—Convert text files to Macintosh format" preference set to **never**. Unpacking the Macintosh download creates a new folder (entitled Squeak3.x) that contains the necessary Squeak files. The newly created folder will look like Figure 1–1 on a Macintosh.

Does it matter which platform I use? Is there one that will be better for using Squeak?

If you browsed the "Downloading Squeak" section on the Squeak Home Page, you probably noticed the amazing range of Squeak ports that are available. The fact that Squeak is written entirely in Smalltalk means that all of the code that you will read and write while reading this book will run on any system for which there is an available Squeak virtual machine (VM). Squeak will provide you with a very enjoyable cross-platform (or platform-neutral) experience so you can use Unix, Windows, or Macintosh.

Okay. Once Squeak is downloaded, how do I get started?

Starting the Squeak environment is done in the same manner as starting any piece of software that's specific to your own computer environment. For example, on a Macintosh or a Microsoft Windows (95/98/NT/2000) machine, you can double click the image file (named Squeak3.0.image) or drag it onto the VM file (Squeak 3.0Alpha8MT on a Macintosh

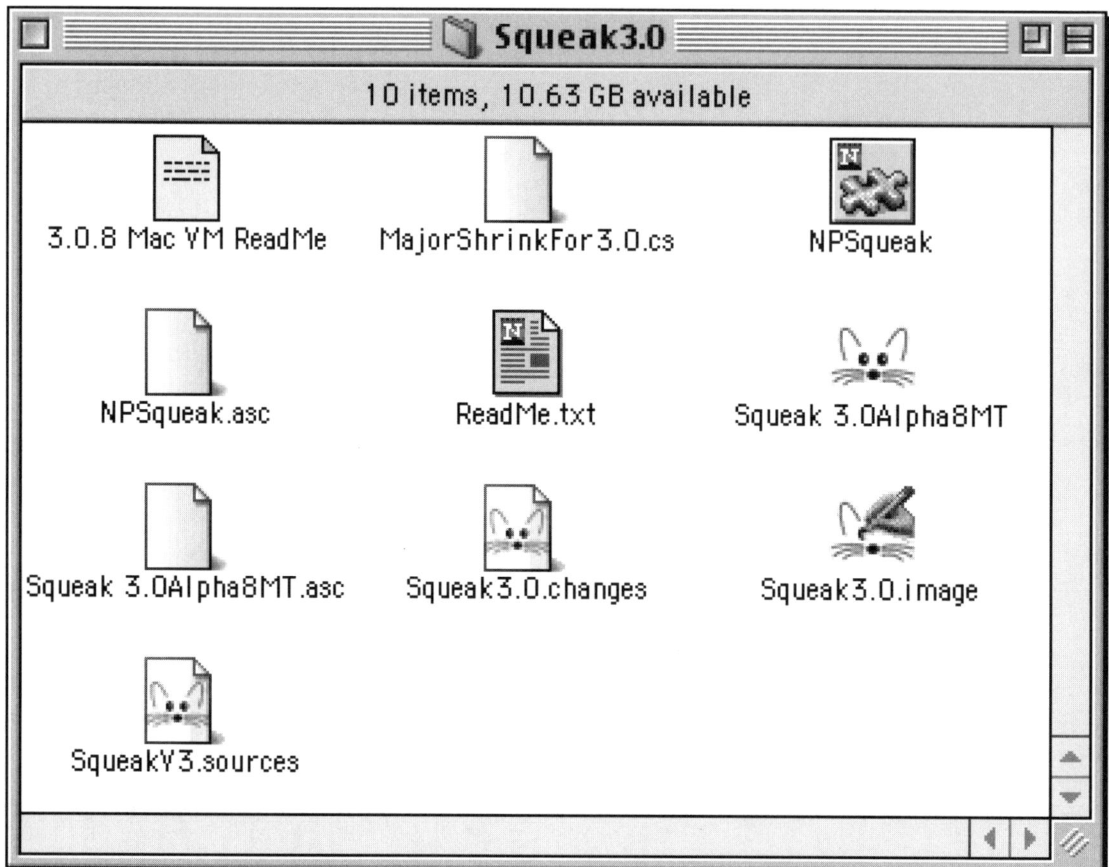

Figure 1–1 The Squeak folder

and just Squeak on a Windows machine). On a Linux box (or some other flavor of Unix), you can type the name of the Squeak executable followed by the name of the image file on the command line.

That sounds easy enough. When I start the Squeak environment, what will I see?

If this is your first time looking at Squeak, Jim, you will note that it looks very much like a conventional, GUI-based application. There's a good reason for this: many of the user interface ideas that we now take for granted originated in Smalltalk.

JIM

This is starting to get complicated. Do I need to know all the information from these two windows right away?

OBJECTIVE LIBRARIAN

After starting Squeak for the first time, you'll be greeted by the Squeak environment running in a window. It should look like the image in Figure 1–2.

The first item that you will notice is a window whose border says **Welcome to....** This window and the minimized window entitled **Getting Started...** contain some general background information about Squeak and resources to consult on the Web.

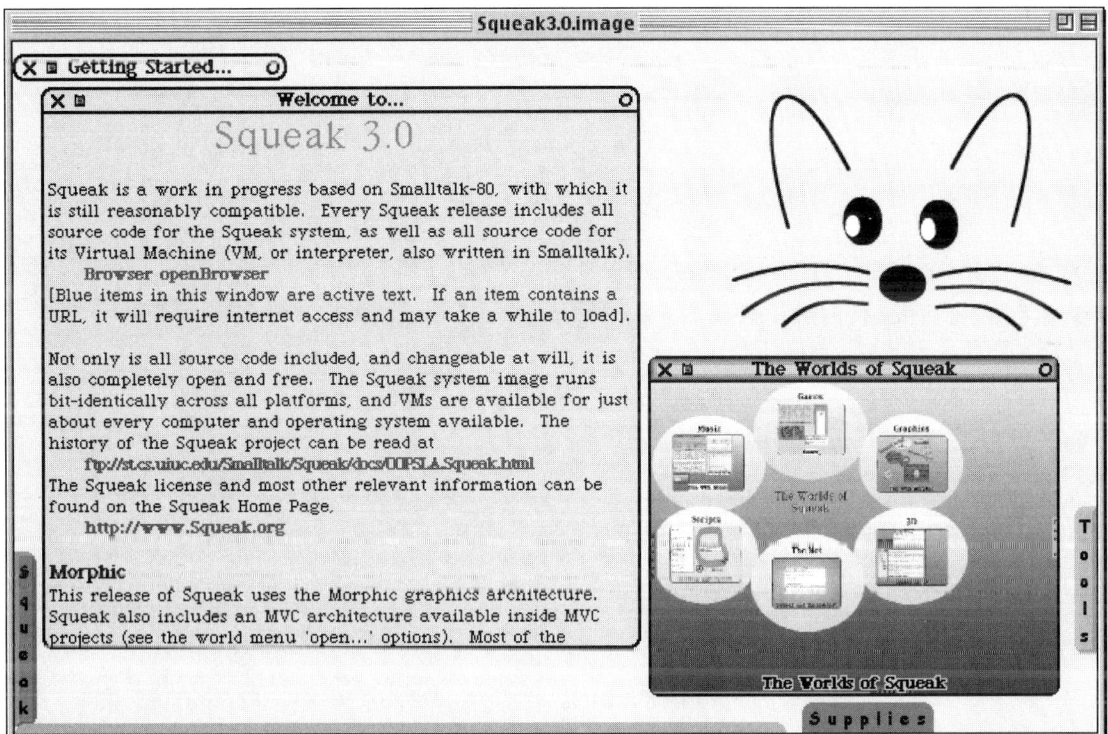

Figure 1–2 The Squeak environment window

Jim	Objective Librarian
	You probably don't need to know too much of this information at the moment, but if you're feeling adventurous, by all means go ahead and read it now. Otherwise, you can come back to it later because there's some really swell stuff included there. You'll want to read these windows at some point. For instance, the Web sites listed in the **Getting Started...** window are invaluable resources.
Okay, I'll hold off for now. What's next?	
	Jim, I can see you're anxious to get started, and that's fabulous. Let's look at the start-up screen more closely. As you move around the start-up screen in a clockwise fashion, the next thing that you should notice occupies a prominent piece of screen real estate in the upper right-hand corner. This little cartoon creature with whiskers is the Squeak mascot. Note how the eyes follow the movement of the cursor.
Wow, that's neat.	
	Just beneath the Squeak image is a **Morphic project** called the **The Worlds of Squeak**. We shall have more to say about Morphic projects in the future. The Worlds of Squeak project is comprised of six subprojects: Games, Graphics, 3D, The Net, Scripts, and Music. Each one pertains to a specific aspect of Squeak's potential. You should definitely take the time to investigate each of them at some point. For now, however, we will be moving in another direction.
Good. In fact, I've heard that Squeak uses a three-button mouse, and, of course, my laptop doesn't have one.	
	That's exactly what you need to know before we go on. Like any other GUI-based software application that you're used to working with—Web browser, word processor, spreadsheet, and so on—the primary means of controlling the Squeak environment is by directing the cursor via the mouse. (For the sake of expediency, I'll generically refer to whatever type of pointing device that you are using—trackball, trackpad, mouse, and so on—as a mouse.) The windows in the

)BJECTIVE LIBRARIAN

‹ just as you think they should. Clicking in ner of the border of a window minimizes ıpper left corner dismisses a window.

a bit of history for you. I'm quite a history ılly.

ıalltalk on which Squeak is based— s designed to be used with a three-button ginal Xerox Smalltalk-80 workstations, uttons was given a primary color: red, yel- ›ntly, the notion of red, yellow, and blue ıming convention.

ısed to select information with the cursor. The yellow button is used to get a menu for working with the contents of a window. The blue button is used to get a menu for manipulating the window itself.

But my mouse doesn't have colored buttons. What do I do?

Since most current computers only ship with a one- or two-button mouse—and the buttons on a three-button mouse are not usually colored red, yellow, and blue—a set of mouse button mappings has been developed for different platforms. Much of the available Squeak literature describes mouse button actions in a manner that's appropriate to the platform that the author is using. In an effort to remain as platform neutral as possible—and in deference to the creators of Smalltalk—I still use the original red, yellow, blue scheme. You'll need to translate to the appropriate action for your own environment. But I'll help you out. Table 1–1 shows the mapping of the red, yellow, and blue buttons to one-, two-, and three-button mice.

That's great, Objective Librarian. I think I'll keep a copy of this table on my desk. That way, I don't have to memorize

Table 1–1 Three-button mouse mapping

	Red	*Yellow*	*Blue*
Macintosh (one button)	Button	Option key + button	Command key + button
Windows (two button)	Left button	Right button	Alt key + right button
Unix (three button)	Left button	Middle button	Right button

the mouse actions for each platform I might use at the office. What's next?

Before we get too far along, we need to discuss how to save and exit from your running Squeak environment. Let's try a little experiment.

Okay, I've got Squeak running, and I'm ready to try anything you suggest. By the way, I was wondering if you are seeing anyone. I'm a single guy, and you're smart as the dickens, and—

Though I see where you're going, Jim, remember that I am an object and have no message interface for a date request. It's evident that testosterone is an unreliable feature. So, shall we get back on task?

Yes, of course. What's next?

Go ahead and mess up your formerly pristine environment.

Are you making fun of me?

No, Jim, your Squeak environment—make a mess of what's on the screen. You should move some of the windows to new positions. Minimize an open window. Maximize a closed window.

Are you sure you want me doing this? What's the point of moving windows, anyway?

JIM	OBJECTIVE LIBRARIAN
	Settle down. I'm showing you some swell things you need to keep in mind when you decide to save work. Next, you need to yellow-button click in an empty section of the Squeak environment (that is, not over a Squeak window). This action will bring up the following menu. This menu, shown in Figure 1–3, is the **World** menu for a Morphic world.
	Let's concentrate on the last four choices.
Okay, those terms are familiar.	
	In our experiment, we should choose the **quit** menu item. This will result in a **Save changes before quitting?** prompt. Choose the **no** option. Now you can go ahead and restart Squeak.

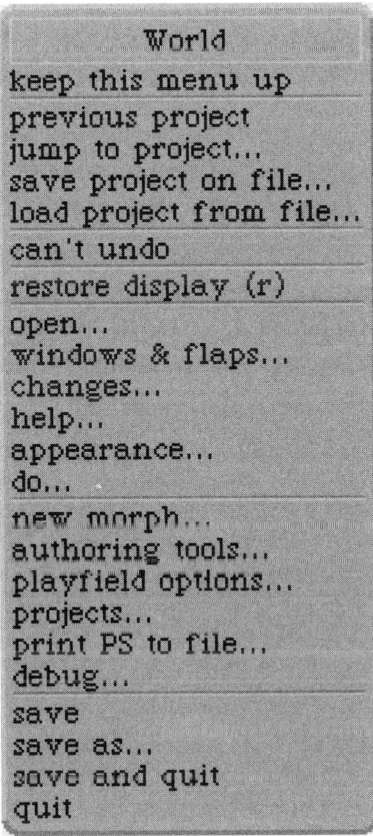

Figure 1–3 World menu for a Morphic world

JIM	OBJECTIVE LIBRARIAN
Hey, the environment appears exactly as it did the very first time that it was started up. But what if I want to save my changes?	
	If you make changes to the environment and use the **save and quit** menu option instead of **quit**, when we restart the environment it will appear as it was when we exited. This can be very handy. For instance, if you must stop working on an application, you can save the current state of the environment and return to it at a later time.
Okay, we're on a roll. What about **save as...**?	
	This menu option will allow you to save your environment under a new name.
Does it work pretty much the same way as in other applications I already use?	
	It's very similar, Jim. When you select this option, a **New File Name?** dialogue appears. In our case, since we haven't done a previous **save as...**, the name **Squeak3.0.image** will appear as the default. Go ahead and rename the image file according to your personal naming convention. This action will result in a new image file and a new changes file. Now, if you should ever run into problems with your Squeak image, you will still have the ability to start and run Squeak by using the original image and changes files.
That will come in handy. And **save** will work just like in other applications?	
	Yes, clearly you understand. So, let's talk about Morphic. From the moment that you started up Squeak—without even knowing it—you have been working with the Morphic user interface. Morphic is one of the two user interfaces available in Squeak. The other Squeak user interface is known as MVC. MVC stands for Model-View-Controller. The Model-

JIM | OBJECTIVE LIBRARIAN

View-Controller user interface paradigm began in the Smalltalk world. MVC and its variants have grown to become the dominant user interface paradigm in existence today. I could go on and on about that.

Nonetheless, the Morphic user interface has become the standard for Squeak. In light of this fact, the Objective Wizard has asked that I focus on Morphic. If you are really interested in using MVC, there are plenty of references available in both print-based and Web-based media.

That's good to keep in mind, but let's open a Morphic project now.

Okay, go ahead and open a new Morphic project and enter it. Just red-button click on an empty space to bring up the **World** menu. Choose the **open** menu item. A graphic image like the one in Figure 1–4 will appear.

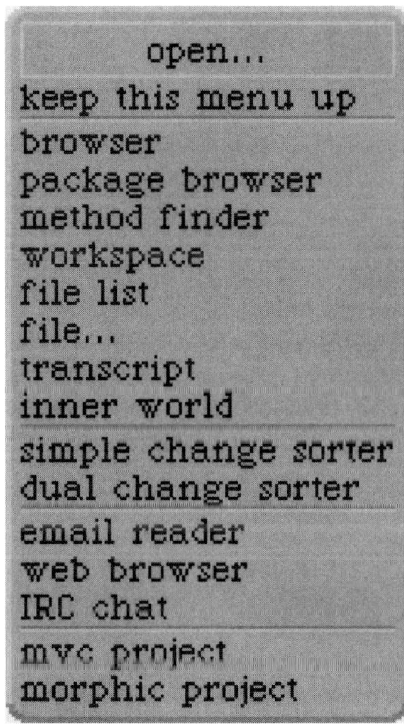

Figure 1–4 The open menu

JIM	OBJECTIVE LIBRARIAN
Okay, I'm following you. Which item should I select?
	Select the **morphic project** item from the menu. This action will result in the creation of the **Unnamed1** Morphic project, as shown in Figure 1–5.
Does the project need a name?
	Yes, you will want to rename this project. Go ahead and select the **Unnamed1** label along the bottom of the window. As is shown in the window below, the Unnamed1 string will be highlighted in green, and the entire window—with the exception of the border—will be surrounded by a light-blue square, as shown in Figure 1–6. Change the highlighted label name to ObjectLand. The resulting Morphic world will look like the image in Figure 1–7.

Figure 1–5 A Morphic project

Figure 1–6 Highlighted Morphic project

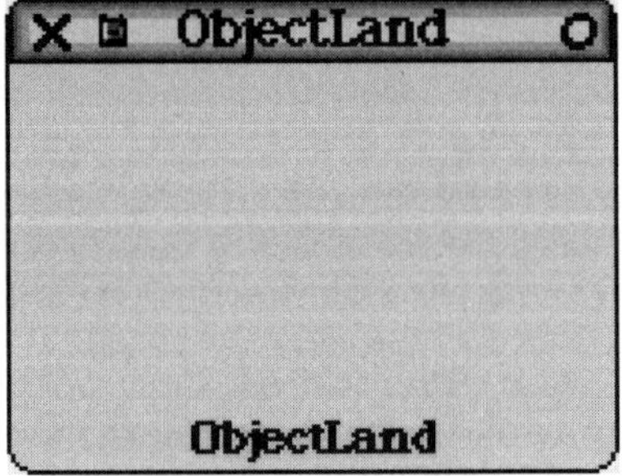

Figure 1–7 The ObjectLand Morphic project

JIM	OBJECTIVE LIBRARIAN

Jim: Got it. Let's enter.

Objective Librarian: To enter the Morphic world, simply red-button click and release somewhere inside the world's borders. This action will cause the Morphic world to fill the entire Squeak environment.

If you bring up the **World** menu again, you will see that returning to the **previous project** is one of the available actions. In fact, a wide variety of project management actions are available from the **World** menu. I'll have more to say about that in just a moment. For now, go ahead and select the **previous project** menu item and observe the results.

Jim: When I do that, I end up in the starting Squeak environment.

Objective Librarian: That's right.

Jim: I'm getting hungry. Can I grab a sandwich before we go on?

Objective Librarian: Yes, take a break if you must, but we have a lot left to cover in the library.

Jim: Munch, munch, gulp, gulp.

Okay, let's get back to the ObjectLand Morphic world now.

Objective Librarian: Okay, Jim. When we were describing the start-up screen for Squeak, we skipped over a couple of items. You can see that those items are present without other distractions in the image in Figure 1–8.

There are three labeled tabs—**Squeak**, **Supplies**, and **Tools**—and a toolbar.

Jim: What do the tabs do?

Objective Librarian: The Squeak tab contains a variety of useful information about the system. Some of the more useful things included among this information are a system clock, a trash can, an **about this system** button, and yet another way to navigate among projects. The Supplies tab contains a set of Morphic components that can be added to a project. The Tools tab

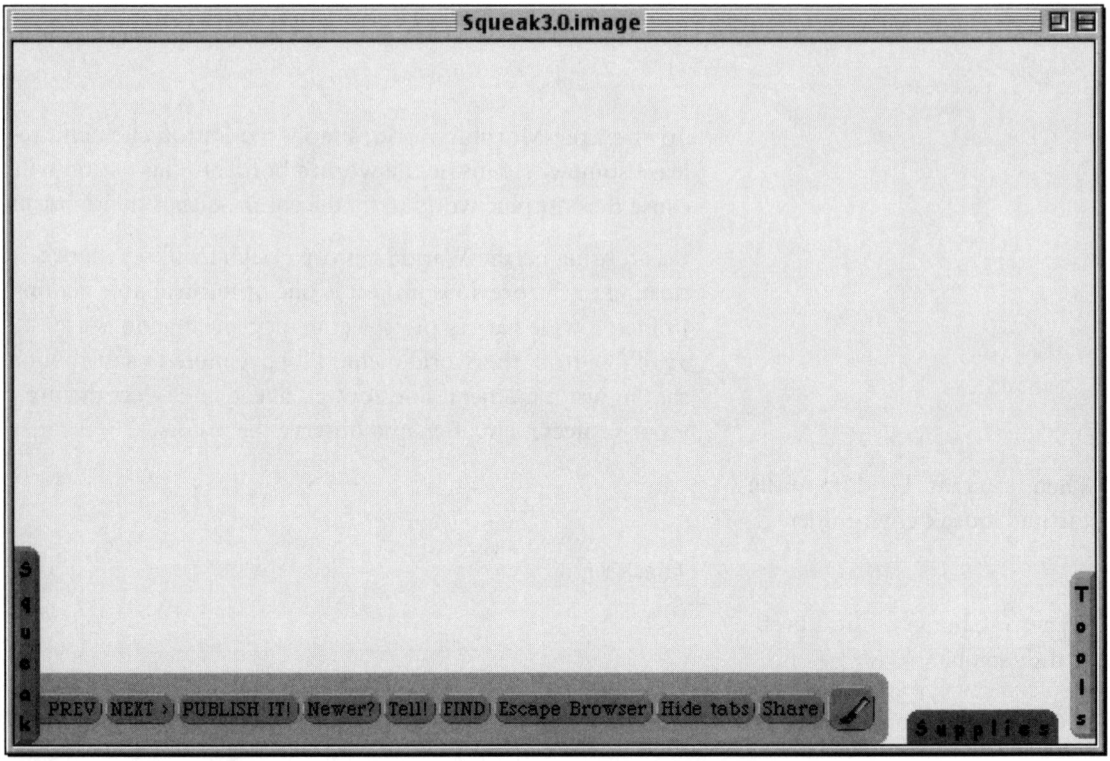

Figure 1–8 Screen showing Squeak, Supplies, and Tool tabs and a toolbar

allows you to access graphically many of the tools that, as you will see later, are available from the Morphic **open...** menu.

The toolbar is called the Project Navigator toolbar. The Project Navigator toolbar is shown by itself in Figure 1–9.

As was mentioned above, the Morphic **World** menu contains a variety of items for managing and moving among your

Figure 1–9 Project Navigator toolbar

JIM	OBJECTIVE LIBRARIAN
	projects. Much of this same functionality is duplicated in the Project Navigator. You should choose a method that is comfortable for you.
	Finally, if you have been very observant, you probably noticed that the Morphic **World** menu has a menu item entitled **windows & flaps...**. Flaps are the same as tabs.
Okay, tell me about some tools.	
	Smalltalk has long been used for successful prototyping of new applications and tools. This ability is a direct result of Smalltalk's interactive, tool-based development environment. The first two tools that we will investigate are the Workspace and the Transcript.
What is the Workspace used for?	
	The Workspace is used to evaluate and test new pieces of code by interacting with the Smalltalk environment itself.
And the Transcript?	
	The Transcript can be used to display the results of the evaluation and testing process.
These two tools seem very important. So, how do I begin to prototype with them?	
	This kind of interactive development is very much akin to the "poke-it-with-a-stick" methodology that humans learn as children. Being a human child sounds like a swell existence, so I like to make use of the reference texts I have acquired on the subject. A favorite pastime of childhood, let's say, is wandering in the woods behind one's house. On encountering something new and unusual that a kid wouldn't want to touch, most children will poke it with a stick to see what, if anything, will happen.
That sounds easy enough. Go on.	
	When prototyping with Squeak, we can take advantage of the same methodological approach by substituting the

JIM	OBJECTIVE LIBRARIAN
	Workspace for the stick and using the Transcript window as a place to record our observations.
I'm not sure I get it. Tell me more about the Workspace.	
	The Workspace functions much as any other simple text editor, perhaps even more simply than many. However, it has the great advantage that it is able to manipulate the running Squeak system directly. As a result, all of the classes and instantiated objects that make up the Squeak runtime are available for you to play with. First, you need to open a Workspace.
How do I do that?	
	As we discussed earlier, one possible way to do this would be to use the Tools flap. Another method for opening a Workspace is from the menus. Try that. Open a Morphic **World** menu by red-button clicking. Choose **open...** from the **World** menu. Select **workspace** from the list of menu items available on the **open...** menu. Now, you can enter and evaluate Smalltalk code in the Workspace. Why don't you enter the expression **3 + 4** and highlight it in the Workspace by red-button clicking at the beginning of the line, as shown in Figure 1–10?
Okay. Go on.	
	The selected expression can be executed—referred to as a "do it" by Smalltalkers—with a blue-button click in the highlighted area. This will bring up the menu shown in Figure 1–11. As indicated in Figure 1–11, you should select **print it (p)**.
Why choose **print it**?	
	Choosing **print it (p)** instead of **do it (d)** will, in addition to executing the statement, print the returned value in the Workspace. The result of this action is shown in Figure 1–12.

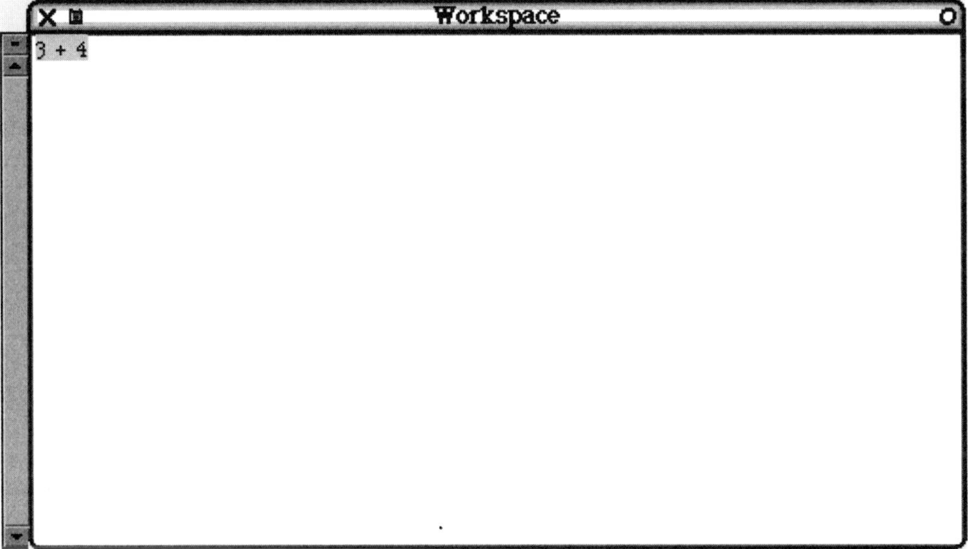

Figure 1–10 Addition in a Workspace

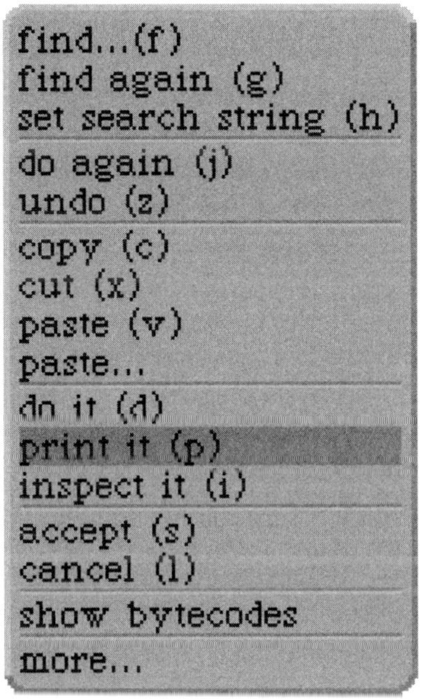

find...(f)
find again (g)
set search string (h)
do again (j)
undo (z)
copy (c)
cut (x)
paste (v)
paste...
do it (d)
print it (p)
inspect it (i)
accept (s)
cancel (l)
show bytecodes
more...

Figure 1–11 Using the "blue–button" menu to do a "print it"

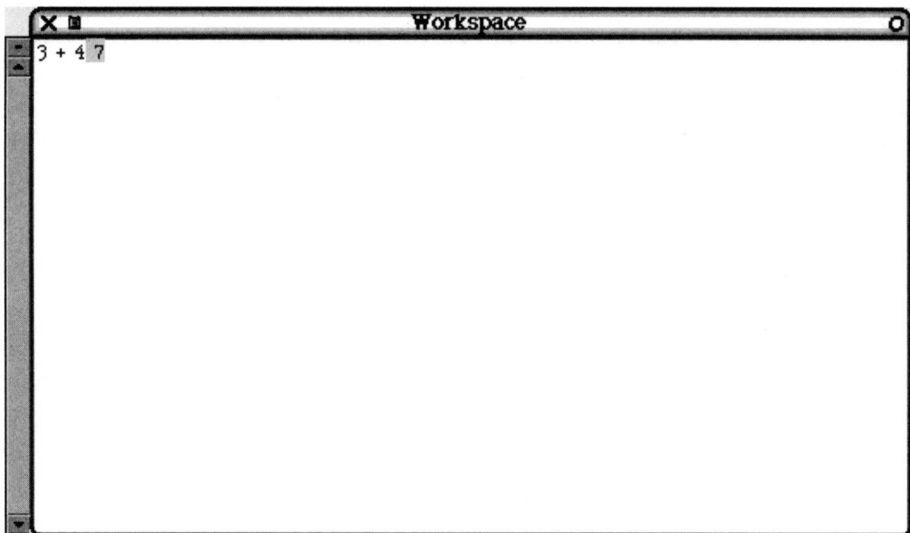

Figure 1–12 Addition results shown in a Workspace

I'm not sure I completely get the Workspace, but what about the Transcript?

The Transcript can be thought of as a simple interface for viewing output. As always, opening a new window, in this case a Transcript, can be accomplished from the Morphic **open** menu. In this instance, select the **transcript** menu item. In order to see how to use the Transcript, you will first enter some Smalltalk code into the Workspace. Next, select and do a **print it...** on the code that you just entered into the window, and you will see the image in Figure 1–13.

I'm not sure I'm getting everything here.

It isn't necessary for you to understand everything that's going on in the highlighted Smalltalk code. For the moment, it's enough to realize that the results of the code that you just executed are being displayed in the Transcript.

Okay, I see that.

Look at the image in Figure 1–14 to double-check your own experiment.

Figure 1–13 Sending messages to the Transcript

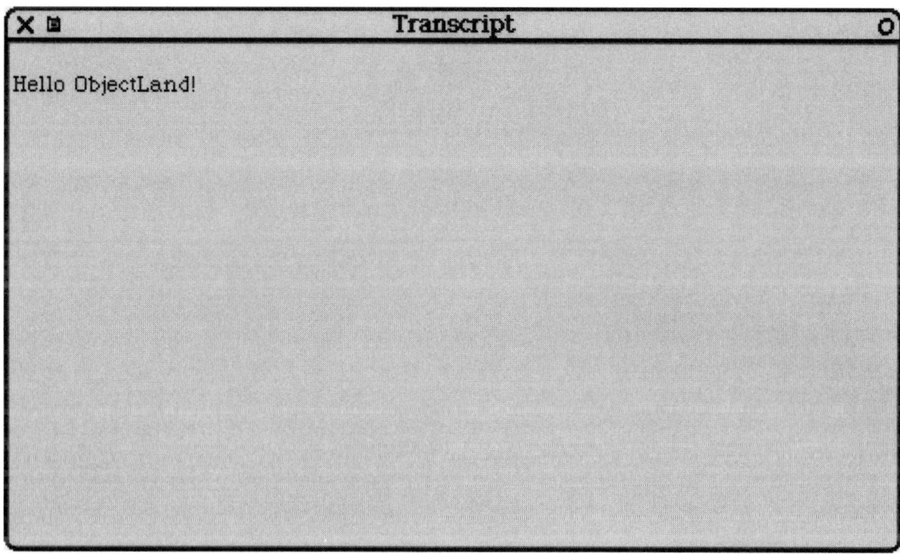

Figure 1–14 Results shown in the Transcript

JIM	OBJECTIVE LIBRARIAN
Can I play around with sending other messages in the Transcript window?	
	Sure, that's a fabulous idea. To send other messages, you need to replace the **Hello ObjectLand!** part of the Smalltalk code with your new message. Make sure that whatever you want to appear in the Transcript is placed between single quotation marks.
I think it's time for me to head out of the library.	
	Yes, I can see you've had enough for now. I had a great time, in object terms, that is. Just remember that you can use the two tools—workspace and Transcript—to develop and test new classes and methods while having the running application at your fingertips as you build the application itself. You'll see more examples of how to do this when you return to ObjectLand. I hope that your first experience in getting to know Squeak has been a rewarding one.

Summary

New Terms

Morphic	Morphic Project
World Menu	Red Button
Workspace	Yellow Button
Transcript	Blue Button

What Did You Learn?

- How to install Squeak on a Windows, Unix, or Macintosh computer.
- How to start the Squeak environment.
- How to adapt Squeak's three-button mouse map to any platform.
- How to save, save as, save and quit, and quit in the Squeak environment.
- How to name a project.
- What the basic functions of the Workspace and the Transcript are.

Words of Wisdom

The Squeak environment is easy to install on any Windows, Unix, or Macintosh computer. It's very important to understand how the mouse on your computer works with the Squeak three-button mouse map.

Remember that there are several different ways to save your work.

Also remember that the Workspace and the Transcript are very important tools to understand in order to prototype new applications and tools. The Workspace functions as a text editor to evaluate and test new pieces of code, and the Transcript displays the results.

To Do List

In the opening window of the Squeak environment, there was a smaller window entitled **Getting Started....** If you have not already done so, go back and read the contents of that window. Use the Scamper Web browser to follow the URL links.

Do the same for the window labeled **Welcome to....**

Investigate the window entitled **The Worlds of Squeak**. Take the time to poke around in each of the six projects. This poke-it-with-a-stick approach will help you to acquaint yourself with the Squeak environment as quickly as possible.

2

ObjectLand

Contents at: 'Chapter 2'

Questions of Interest

- What is a class?
- What is an instance?
- What is a message?
- What is a method?

- How do methods and messages relate?
- What does Squeak code look like?
- How do I read Squeak code?

Introduction

Welcome to ObjectLand!

This is where your journey into the object-oriented paradigm begins. In this chapter we will learn these fundamental object-oriented concepts: object, class, message, and method. Because Smalltalk is a class-based implementation of an object-oriented language, we will also learn the significance of class and instance and their roles in implementation.

Most of you have some experience with solving problems by using programming languages, and all of this experience has value. The object-oriented paradigm, the Smalltalk language, and the Squeak environment, however, are significantly different and should be approached as something new, rather than as just another paradigm, another programming language, another environment. Avoid making comparisons between what you already know about programming and what you are about to learn.

Goals for This Chapter

- To understand and be able to work with the following concepts:

  Object
  Class
  Instance
  Message
  Method

- To learn how to read Smalltalk code. After all, reading code is the first step toward writing code.

When you are finished with this chapter, you will know about objects and, more importantly, you will have begun to think in terms of objects, classes, and messages. With effort, you will begin to see the world around you as consisting of objects passing messages and executing methods.

JIM	OBJECTIVE WIZARD
This looks familiar. Is this downtown Austin, Texas?	
	You are back in ObjectLand, a virtual world in the Squeak environment that exists to simulate what you call the real world. You know that ObjectLand is made up of objects. You need to update your memory chips, Jim. How is your recollection?
ObjectLand, got it!	
	The objects here communicate with one another by sending messages. We accomplish things in ObjectLand by creating appropriate objects, telling them what messages they can respond to, and telling them how to respond to a given message with methods.
Is that all?	
	No, there is much more to ObjectLand, but that will take time to explain. Be patient. In a short time, you will know much more. After all, you have just begun your visits here.
Okay, no smoke and mirrors. Tell me *exactly* what an object is.	
	An *object* is an item in the real world. You are an object, and so am I. Your pen, car, television, and so on are objects. Objects can also be design entities in a software design document and implementation entities in an application, as you will learn in later chapters. An *object* in Smalltalk is an implementation-level model of an object from the real or design world. A Squeak object can be described as a conceptual entity that has a private inside and a public outside. The inside of an object contains information in variables. This private inside—this state—can be accessed only by a message from the outside. Each object understands and responds to a particular set of messages; each message activates a method that results in some behavior.
You said that I am an object, didn't you?	

JIM | OBJECTIVE WIZARD

Objective Wizard: In a manner of speaking, yes. What are you getting at?

Jim: I'm trying to understand the Smalltalk way of thinking. If I am an object, then maybe I have internal states and external behaviors.

Objective Wizard: Well, in a manner of speaking, yes. Be careful about making too simple a comparison, though. We are trying to understand objects here; we are not trying to understand your individual, human psyche.

Jim: Right, but if I'm an object, then maybe a message is like when my boss asks me when a project will be done. I always return an unrealistic but satisfactory date. Am I on the right track?

Objective Wizard: In some sense, you are—but, Jim, I think you are trying to fit object-oriented thinking into your preexisting paradigm that allows you to understand yourself. Again, you need to resist that tendency.

Jim: Okay, then, how about some other examples of objects?

Objective Wizard: Okay. Let us imagine a drawing implement in ObjectLand. A pen object.

A usable pen object must have a point or nib. It must also have a location, a direction, and something that stores its up/down state. It needs a drawing surface, of course, but that sounds like a different object to me.

In Squeak, this pen object would be implemented as a `Pen` class, and the nib, location, direction, and up/down state would be stored as variables in that object.

Jim: Variables?

Objective Wizard: The variables would also contain objects. For example, the location probably would refer to a point on the drawing sur-

JIM | OBJECTIVE WIZARD

face; the direction might be expressed in terms of an integer number of degrees from direction 0 degrees. In both cases, these references are—and must be—implemented as objects. Points are objects that internally store values for *x*- and *y*-coordinates. Integers are also objects.

Hmm, so a pen object is a thing that stores, in variables, the information it needs to do its job?

Yes!

Do objects really know things?

No, but you will find that we in ObjectLand always give objects more credit than they deserve for knowing what they are doing. We have found that, by thinking in terms of intelligent objects, we design more intelligent objects.

Think about it.

You used the term *class*?

The term *object* refers to the conceptual entity we have been talking about; in Squeak, however, objects with common characteristics are defined as a *class*, which simply means a group of similar objects.

So, pen is a class, really. How is a class used?

The class contains the definition for the object. The information inside the object is described in the class definition. The class also has the ability to create an instance of itself when it receives the new message.

Instance? What's that?

An *instance* is an object and is defined by its class definition. Most of the objects you will work with when implementing in Smalltalk will be instances of some class. You will occasionally work directly with a class.

Message? Could you explain that to me, please?

JIM	OBJECTIVE WIZARD
	Yes. Conceptually, a *message* is a request sent to an object, the *receiver object,* by another object called the *sender object.* The request always results in an action performed by the execution of a method. The set of messages that an object will respond to is called its *message interface* because an object's messages are its interface to the outside world of other objects.
Method?	
	Yes, a *method* is a piece of Smalltalk code. It consists of one or more Smalltalk expressions. Every message, when it is received by an object, activates a method. Methods are always associated with a particular class of objects.
Okay, but—one more time—could you tell me what an object is?	
	Sure. An *object* is an encapsulated package of information and descriptions of the manipulation of that information. In some ways, it can be thought of as a combined chunk of data and procedure. In another way, it can be thought of as a small computer having its own protected memory and its own set of functions to act on the contents of its memory. An object in Smalltalk is always either a class or an instance. In either case, the definition of what that object does is defined in the class. The class definition consists of a list of the following information: class variable names instance variable names pool dictionaries class methods instance methods
How about an example of a class definition?	
	Sure!

JIM	OBJECTIVE WIZARD
	The Pen object, which we discussed just moments ago, is a good example. The first step would be to implement it as a class called Pen. The Pen class definition would look like the list here:

class name:	Pen
instancevariable names:	location
	direction
	penDown
class variable names:	none
pool dictionaries:	none

The remainder of the class definition is a list of messages that the class and instances can receive and of the associated methods with which the class and its instances will respond. This remaining part of the class definition is really two different lists, one for the class and one for the instances of the class.

JIM: How can I create an instance of class Pen?

OBJECTIVE WIZARD: Easy. Send the new message to the class Pen. The Smalltalk code would look like this:

```
Pen new.
```

This sort of message is the essential, first step in creating any instance of a class.

JIM: Okay, let me see if I have this right. What you are saying is that the fundamental programming unit of Smalltalk is the object and that the object contains information in class, instance, and those pool things.

OBJECTIVE WIZARD: Pool variables, but do not worry about them now.

JIM: Objects do programmed behavior when a message is sent to

JIM | OBJECTIVE WIZARD

Jim: them. They subsequently execute the corresponding method code.

Objective Wizard: Technically speaking, yes.

Jim: What happens after the method code is finished executing?

Objective Wizard: An action of some sort may have occurred, based on what the method code was written to do, but an object is always returned to the sending expression.

Jim: Huh?

Objective Wizard: Every message send results in an object that is returned to the expression that sent the message.

Jim: Huh?

Objective Wizard: The fundamental unit of Smalltalk code is called an *expression*. An expression consists of one or more message sends to objects. Consider the following expression:

```
'Squeak is easy' size
```

What you just read is real Smalltalk code. It reads: send the `size` message to the string object `'Squeak is easy'`. This message send will return the integer object `14` because the `size` message sent to a string object will answer (return) an integer that is the number of characters in the string. Let us try a slightly more complex expression, as follows:

```
'Squeak is easy' asSet size
```

This expression reads: send the `asSet` message to the string object `'Squeak is easy'` and then send the `size` message to the set object returned from the `asSet` message send. This expression will return the integer object `10` because the `asSet` message returns a set object (because sets cannot contain redundant elements). The size message then is sent to the returned set object and answers an integer that is the number of characters in the set.

Jim: This is very different from what I am used to, but I can almost understand it!

JIM	OBJECTIVE WIZARD

Objective Wizard: Soon, that expression will be baby talk to you. (Oops, I sent a Squeak Smalltalk joke message.)

Jim: Ha, ha! Okay, a message send always returns an object, and an expression is a chunk of code that is made of one or more message sends. A method is one or more expressions, right?

Objective Wizard: Yes, and in every message send there is a message and a receiver object. The object to which the message is sent is referred to as the *receiver object*, and the object that sends the message is called the *sender object*.

For future reference, you may want to know that the receiver object is stored in the pseudo variable `self`. You can access `self` and use it in your code. I, or perhaps the Objective Librarian, will discuss it again later.

Jim: Give me another example. And this time, talk in terms of class, instance, class variables, and instance variables.

Objective Wizard: Okay. Let us build a piece of paper for our pen to write on. A usable paper object must have a height, a width, and a location that describes where it is. It must also contain the information that is drawn on it.

Note that, in Squeak, this paper object would probably be implemented in a more general form of drawing medium. In ObjectLand, we usually seek out general solutions to problems, then specialize our general solution to fit a particular need. We find that this approach helps us to reuse the general portion of our solution in each of the specializations. It saves time and promotes an incremental approach to development. However, since you are human and since we have conceptualized a pen object, let us think specifically paper.

Height and width could be integer objects; location could be represented by a point object; and the actual drawn image

JIM	OBJECTIVE WIZARD
	could be represented as a separate object. All of these would be stored as instance variables in every instance of paper. In this particular implementation of paper, there are no class or pool variables. It is not uncommon to create classes that use only instance variables.
I understand to a degree, I guess.	
	The sender always begins by sending the new message, which creates, or returns, the piece of paper to the sender. Then, the sender can send each message; the object—the piece of paper—returns to the sender—to you—what the object knows about itself, such as its width.
Beep, beep, back up the bus. We don't really have a pen and a piece of paper here, and we didn't really create a pen object or a paper object using Smalltalk. I think I need to do the implementation in Smalltalk myself to understand it completely.	
	In many respects, you are correct. However, you are unprepared to create objects in Smalltalk at this juncture. On the other hand, as you humans like to say, we have accomplished important conceptual work. Once you understand the way we in ObjectLand think about objects—in our examples, about pen and paper—you will need to visit our library for an introduction to the basic tools.
So, I'll have the chance to speak with the Objective Librarian again?	
	Yes. Only after discussing tools with the Objective Librarian will you actually be able to use Smalltalk in your Squeak environment. For now, you must prepare a way of thinking so that you can learn about the tools.

JIM	OBJECTIVE WIZARD
Oh. Well, then, we had better go over a few things again.	
	First of all, I should point out that Smalltalk is embedded in the Squeak programming environment. The Squeak environment is what you are using when you bring up Squeak. The programming environment consists of a group of tools, such as the System Browser, the Workspace, and the Transcript, which you can use to do various programming tasks. Most of the programming tools are window based. A window is an object whose job is to display information and get feedback from users such as yourself. Windows almost always have one or more menus associated with them to let the users pick actions they want to have performed.
Oh, yeah. I'm certainly familiar with the idea of a window.	
	You should not have any trouble. It may take some time to get used to the Squeak environment, but windows and other aspects make this environment especially inviting for humans.
Then I should be fine as long as I remember that windows show information and that menus are for choosing actions.	
	It will help if you spend some time every day playing with the environment. But do not do it too loudly—the environment *is* ObjectLand, and you might wake me up.
I'll be careful not to disturb you, Wizard. So, Squeak's the environment, Smalltalk's the language, and pen and paper are examples of objects.	
	Yes, basically. The Objective Librarian soon will introduce you to tools you can use to implement, say, a piece of virtual paper.

JIM	OBJECTIVE WIZARD
Ah, the Objective Librarian.	
	What you need to remember, then, are the basic concepts of class definition and of instance variables.
You mean our list of height, width, location, and so on?	
	Yes, and remember that these characteristics, such as width and color, are instance variables that, because of encapsulation, can be accessed only through the object's message interface. A partial message interface to the paper object might have the following messages:

Message	Activity
`new`	Create a piece of paper
`location`	Answer the location
`move: aPoint`	Change the location
`size`	Answer the size
`height`	Answer the height
`width`	Answer the width
`display`	Display the paper
`color`	Answer the color

JIM	OBJECTIVE WIZARD
	Each item in the list on the right represents the activity that results when the receiving object receives the corresponding message from the left column. So, the first message returns a newly instantiated paper object. Each time a message from the left column is sent, it activates a corresponding method and something is returned to the sending object.
Um, then these are messages that the paper object can receive. When each message is received, the receiving object returns an appropriate object.	
	Yes, the corresponding Smalltalk method code is executed for each message the object receives.
Whew! That's not easy to comprehend. I think I understand,	

Jim

but the more I think about classes and methods, the more I doubt myself.

Objective Wizard

The concepts are not easy, but you now know much of the Smalltalk programming process.

You should tackle the To Do List at the end of this chapter to help you keep thinking in the ways of ObjectLand. Once you feel comfortable thinking about objects, classes, and methods, you are ready to go to the library to learn about some tools.

Summary

New Terms

Object	Class Variable
Message	Instance Variable
Method	Receiver Object
Class	Sender Object
Instance	Expression

What Did You Learn?

- ObjectLand is a weird place.
- The basic concepts of object, class, message, and method.
- The relationship between class and instance.
- The relationship between message and method.
- How to "design"—at least conceptually—a class.

Words of Wisdom

The words *message* and *method* are often, but erroneously, used interchangeably. This mistake is understandable but is one that can be confusing for the novice. Remember that a message is sent from the outside world to an object, whereas a method is something inside the object that is activated by that message.

Classes are classes, and instances are instances—but objects are everything.

To Do List

Think of a real-world object. Keep it simple, perhaps a toothbrush, a postage stamp, or a lipstick if you can't think of one on your own. Write a simple class definition for that real-world object; begin with the class name and include the appropriate variables (characteristics). Then, as this chapter did for `Pen` and for `Paper`, adapt your conceptual class definition to develop a message interface; begin, as always, with `new` and list the appropriate method for each message.

Make a brief list of possible objects—maybe three or four of them—that you might like to create once you know how to use the necessary tools. Keep this list handy so that, as you learn how to write Smalltalk code for the Squeak environment, you can pursue these ideas for objects or perhaps revise your expectations for your own objects as your knowledge increases.

3

A View of the Tools

Contents at: 'Chapter 3'

#(

environment customization
window colors
scrollbars

Morphic
halo
handles

System Browser
categories

finding a class
finding a method

adding a class
adding a category
adding a method

opening a file

filing out

removing a method
removing a class

filing in

goodies).

Questions of Interest

- How do I customize the Squeak environment?
- What are morphs and halos?
- How do I use the System Browser?
- How do I find a class or a method?
- How do I add a class or a method?
- How do I open a file?
- How do I save and retrieve my work?
- How do I remove classes and methods?

Introduction

Welcome back to the library. The Objective Librarian, ObjectLand's knowledgeable librarian, will take you on a tour of very important tasks you will need to understand your work in the Squeak environment.

In this chapter, you will learn how to make your Squeak environment your own by customizing the environment and by creating classes, adding methods, and removing work from the system. You will also learn how to find, open, and retrieve work that is part of your Squeak environment.

Goals for This Chapter

- To familiarize yourself with the Squeak environment and some of its basic functions so that you will be able to create, save, retrieve, and remove your work.
- To begin making the Squeak environment that you had installed on your own computer *your* working environment as a Squeak programmer.
- When you are finished with this chapter, you will know how to do the following tasks:

  Customize the appearance of the environment.
  Use morphs and their halos of icons.
  Use the System Browser.
  Find a class.
  Find a method.
  Create a class.
  Add a method.
  Open a file.
  Save your work and *file out.*
  Remove classes and methods.
  Retrieve your work and the work of others.

JIM	OBJECTIVE LIBRARIAN
Hello, Objective Librarian, it's good to be back in the library.	
	Welcome back, Jim. It's fabulous to see you again. I'd like to start your visit by having a little fun. How does that sound?
Why, Objective Librarian, I thought you'd never ask. I'm certainly interested in having some fun with you.	
	Swell. Before you get started learning more about how to program effectively in the Squeak environment, let's have some fun discovering just how easy it is to customize Squeak. To start, enter a Morphic project.
Okay, although I'm not sure this is the sort of fun I had hoped for.	
	Oh, I think you'll find it great fun. It's certainly the kind of thing I like. First, you should red-button click to bring up a **World** menu. About halfway down the **World** menu, you will find the **appearance...** menu item. Choose it. The resulting **appearance...** menu will look like the screenshot shown in Figure 3–1.

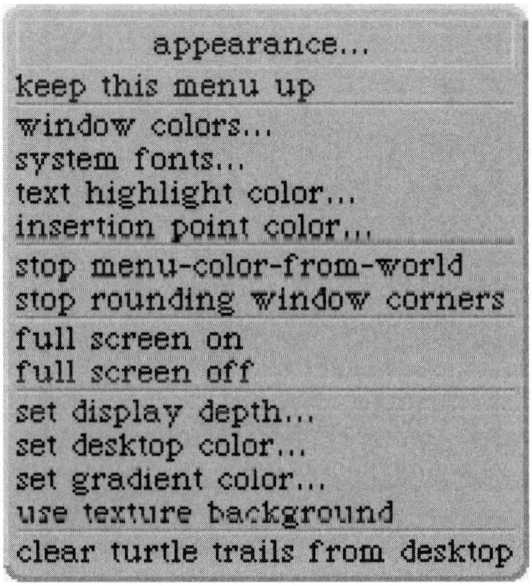

Figure 3–1 Morphic appearance... menu

JIM	OBJECTIVE LIBRARIAN
Hey, it looks like I can change the colors. Let's do that.	
	Okay. I do have information that indicates color is very important to humans, and Squeak tries to address numerous human tendencies such as color preferences.
	If you're unhappy with the default colors that Squeak provides, you can change the colors of the various windows in Squeak via the **window colors...** menu item. If you select **window colors...**, an editing window will pop up, as shown in Figure 3–2 .
Cool. Let me play with the colors for a minute.	
	Jim, let's go on. The chances are, according to my information, that you will choose blue.

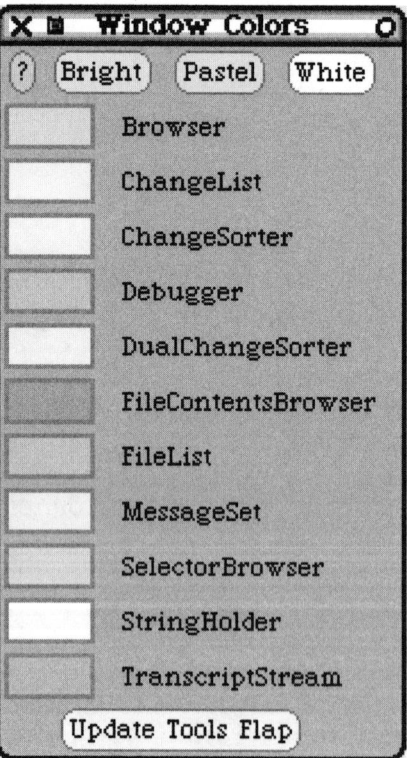

Figure 3–2 The Window Colors window

Jim	Objective Librarian
	Two useful choices can be found in the menu group of the **appearance...** menu. The items **full screen on** and **full screen off** are self-explanatory, but you should try them out anyway. I often like to work in the **full screen on** mode since this maximizes the available screen real estate.
Okay, I'll try that. What about the other two items in that group?	
	You can also modify the shape of Squeak's larger, system-type windows. By selecting the **stop rounding window corners** menu item, as shown in Figure 3–3, windows such as the Transcript and Workspace will be shown with squared-off corners instead of their default, rounded appearance.
Why, there are all sorts of little things I can change just for the fun of it. I think I like the rounded corners.	
	That is a typical human preference. I prefer the squared-off look, and the images that you'll see in the rest of this chapter are shown that way.

appearance...
keep this menu up
window colors...
system fonts...
text highlight color...
insertion point color...
stop menu-color-from-world
stop rounding window corners
full screen on
full screen off
set display depth...
set desktop color...
set gradient color...
use texture background
clear turtle trails from desktop

Figure 3–3 Selecting stop rounding window corners

JIM	OBJECTIVE LIBRARIAN
	Now, on to the scrollbars. By default, the scrollbars appear only when the cursor enters a window. While this behavior can save screen space, I find it distracting, particularly in the case of the System Browser. We haven't discussed the System Browser before, but we'll be taking a closer look at it in a moment.
So, I can get the scrollbars to be there all the time?	
	Yes, Squeak allows you to modify the default behavior so that scrollbars appear in each window at all times. There are two ways to accomplish this. The first way to add scrollbars to each window is by means of the Morphic **help...** menu. You should select **help...** from the **World** menu, as shown in Figure 3–4.
Ah, the **help...** menu sounds like a good one for me to know.	
	On the **help...** menu, select the **preferences...** menu item. This selection will result in a **Preferences** window. Initially, the **general** preferences section will be shown. You need to

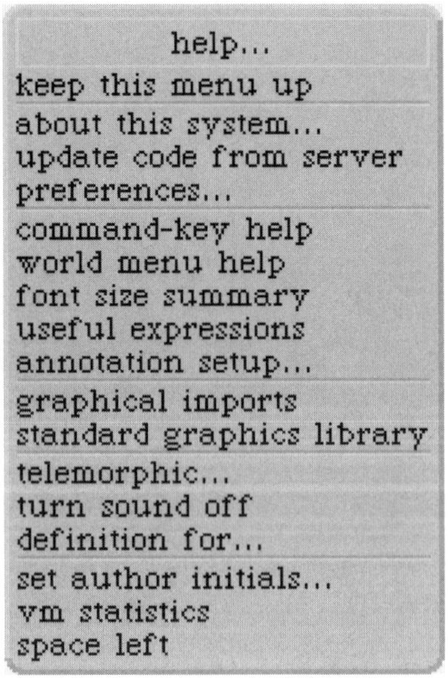

help...
keep this menu up
about this system...
update code from server
preferences...
command-key help
world menu help
font size summary
useful expressions
annotation setup...
graphical imports
standard graphics library
telemorphic...
turn sound off
definition for...
set author initials...
vm statistics
space left

Figure 3–4 Morphic help... menu

JIM

OBJECTIVE LIBRARIAN

change this, as we have demonstrated in the screenshot in Figure 3–5, by first selecting the **scrolling** item. Then, after the options related to scrolling appear, check the **inboard-Scrollbars** option.

How do I know it worked?

You can test for the results of the changes by opening a new Workspace. It'll look like the image in Figure 3–6.

Okay, now you said there was another way to do the same thing?

You can also make this same scrollbar change programmatically. Go back to the **Preferences** window and deselect the **inboardScrollbars** option. Now, go ahead and open a new

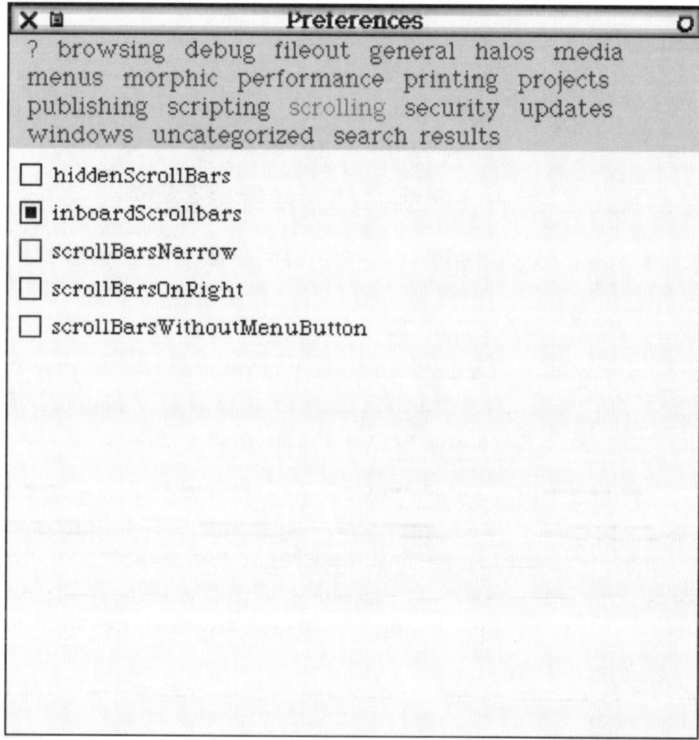

Figure 3–5 The Preferences window

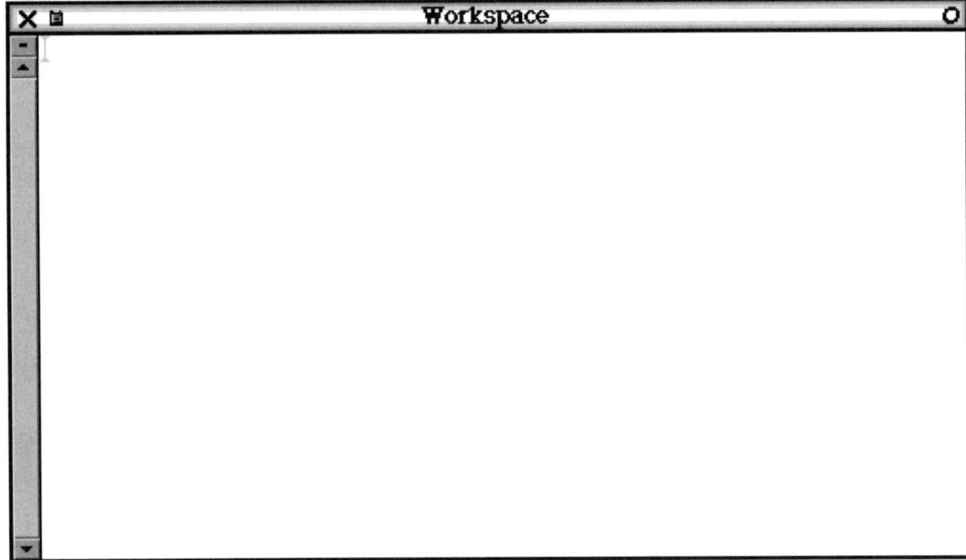

Figure 3–6 A Workspace with square corners

Workspace. Or, you can use the Workspace that you just opened, if you have not already dismissed it. Enter and do a **print it** (**d**) on this Smalltalk expression:

```
Preferences setPreference:
      #inboardScrollbars toValue: true
```

Oops, I had already dismissed the Workspace.

That's fine. Since you opened yet another Workspace, you noticed that this move has had the same effect as making the change via the **Preferences** window.

As you can see from the **Preferences** window in Figure 3–5, there are a great many behaviors that you can customize to your liking. Each of these behaviors can also be modified via the Workspace. We recommend that you use both methods to give you opportunities to experiment with the Squeak environment.

Okay, I'll just grab a quick double espresso and a chocolate bar before I do too much experimenting.

JIM	OBJECTIVE LIBRARIAN
	Are you ready to go on now?
Yes. What's next?	
	Earlier, in your last visit to the library, I mentioned the Morphic user interface in the context of Morphic projects and Morphic worlds. Now seems to be an appropriate moment to say a bit more about Morphic. Back in ObjectLand, there's an entire chapter devoted to Morphic programming and to writing a tiny Morphic application that does some animation, but I'll just whet your appetite for what is to follow.
You'll whet my appetite? Go on.	
	The Morphic system, quite logically, is composed of morphs. A *morph* is a graphical object. Before you leave ObjectLand, you'll have been exposed to several types of morphs, some of which you have already seen without realizing it. Earlier in this visit, you saw the screenshot of a Morphic **help...** menu. Please take note of the difference between the earlier **help...** menu and the one shown in Figure 3–7.

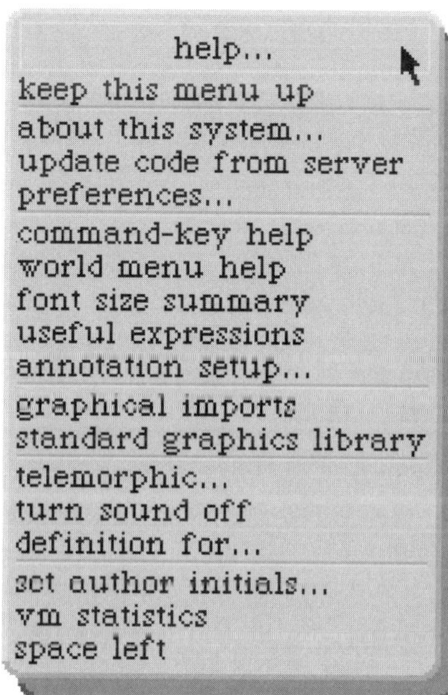

Figure 3–7 Morphic help... menu

Jim	Objective Librarian
Okay, I think I see the difference.	
	The **help...** menu in this image has been selected, and it appears as if it has been lifted off the surface of the screen. By red-button clicking in the blue region of the menu, we can pick up the menu and move it to a new location in the environment. One of the many swell features that the Morphic interface offers users is readily apparent in this graphic. Note the gray shading running down the right side and lower edge of the menu. This shading is used to give the morph the appearance of having been lifted above the surface of the screen. In a cluttered window, this feature can provide you with essential feedback because it's clear whether or not you have grabbed your intended target.
I see. That could be helpful. Now, what are all these tiny things I see around the morph I have?	
	Another feature of morphs is a set of tiny icons that ring the morph; this formation is called a *halo*. The individual icons are actually known as *handles*. Each handle represents a particular function or behavior that you can use to change a morph.
But there are so many. I might need another espresso before we go on.	
	Jim, you're doing just fine, and I think you'll find these handles fun, so let's stay on task. You can activate a morph's halo by blue-button clicking on the morph itself. As you can see in the image in Figure 3–8, activating the morph's halo also causes a text string describing the morph that you have selected. This text string is another example of the morph providing feedback to the user. In this case, we have selected the System Window.

Figure 3–8 The Morphic halo

Although each handle icon contains a small graphic representation that is meant to indicate its function, these symbols can be somewhat confusing if you are a new user. In an attempt to reduce this confusion, each handle provides a clue to its function. Simply place—without selecting—your cursor on a handle, and a description bubble will pop up. If you rest your cursor on the yellow handle in the lower right corner, you'll discover that this handle can be used to change the size of the morph.

Yes, I see.

Since changing the size of a window in a graphical application is one of the more common activities that you'll perform, the utility of this handle is immediately apparent. Another common task in windowing environments is moving a graphical object to a new location. In the Morphic halo, this facility is available from the black icon. This icon contains a graphic that resembles a pair of tongs lifting an object.

JIM | OBJECTIVE LIBRARIAN

Jim: Okay, these handles aren't as daunting as they first seemed. I can see how they will be useful—and, I suppose, fun.

Objective Librarian: You should definitely take some time to experiment with morphs and their respective halos. A wide variety of morphs can be accessed from the **World** menu. If you select the **new morph...** menu item on the **World** menu, the **Add a new morph** menu will be brought up. Some very interesting morphs can be found by selecting either the **Demo** or the **Games** menu item. For now, play with them to your heart's content. You'll find out more about morphs and the Morphic user interface back in ObjectLand.

Jim: Okay, enough of that. I think I'm on a roll. What's next?

Objective Librarian: It should come as no surprise that Smalltalk has a tool—in fact, a variety of tools—for scanning the class hierarchy. In Smalltalk parlance, the act of scanning is referred to as *browsing*. In accordance with this nomenclature, the tool used to do this browsing is called a *browser*.

Jim: Hold on, I'm not sure about *parlance* and *nomenclature*. But I do know what a browser is, sort of.

Objective Librarian: Good enough. The mother of all browsers in the Squeak environment is the System Browser. A System Browser consists of a set of panes for presenting views into the Squeak classes and a text-editing pane for modifying existing code and adding new classes and methods. To open a new instance of a System Browser, select the **open...** menu item from a **World** menu. From the resulting **open...** menu, select **browser** (Figure 3–9).

Jim: What's this list in the corner?

Objective Librarian: The pane in the upper left corner of the System Browser contains a list of categories.

Jim: What's a category?

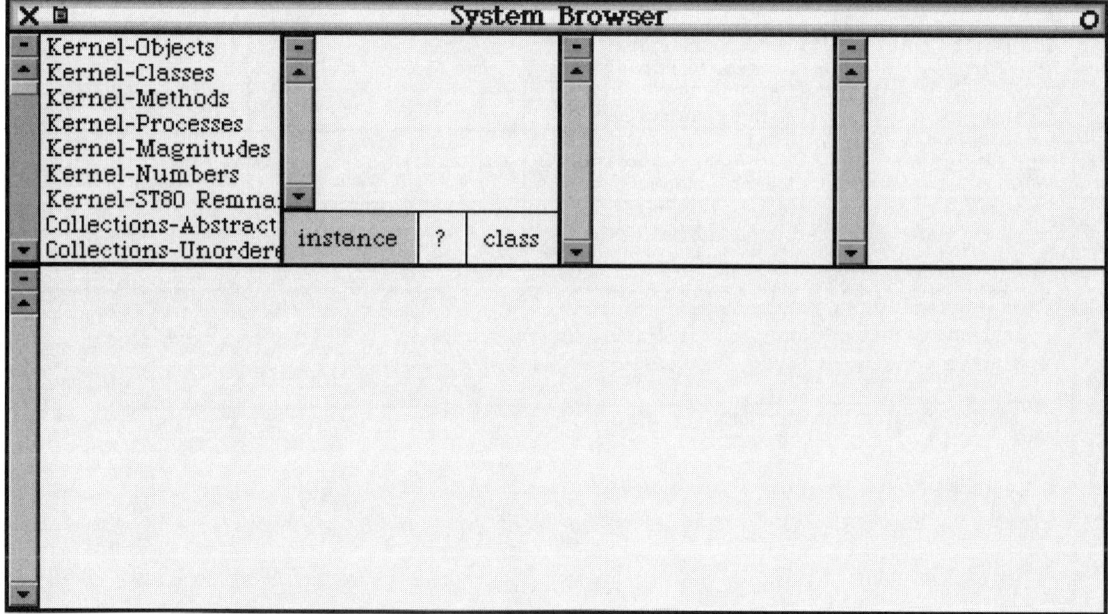

Figure 3–9 The System Browser

Categories are used as organizational tools in Squeak. A category defines a set of related classes. The Squeak system is composed of a great many categories. While we don't have the time or space to cover them all here, back in ObjectLand you'll be exposed to categories such as:

```
Kernel-Magnitude
Kernel-Numbers
Collections-Abstract
Collections-Arrayed
```

Further down the road in this visit, you'll see how to create a new category and how to add a class to that category. But, before we tackle that project, you need to learn how to browse the categories and their associated classes.

Use the scrollbar in the category pane to bring the category **Morphic-Kernel** into view. Once the category is in view, select that category. The result is shown in Figure 3–10.

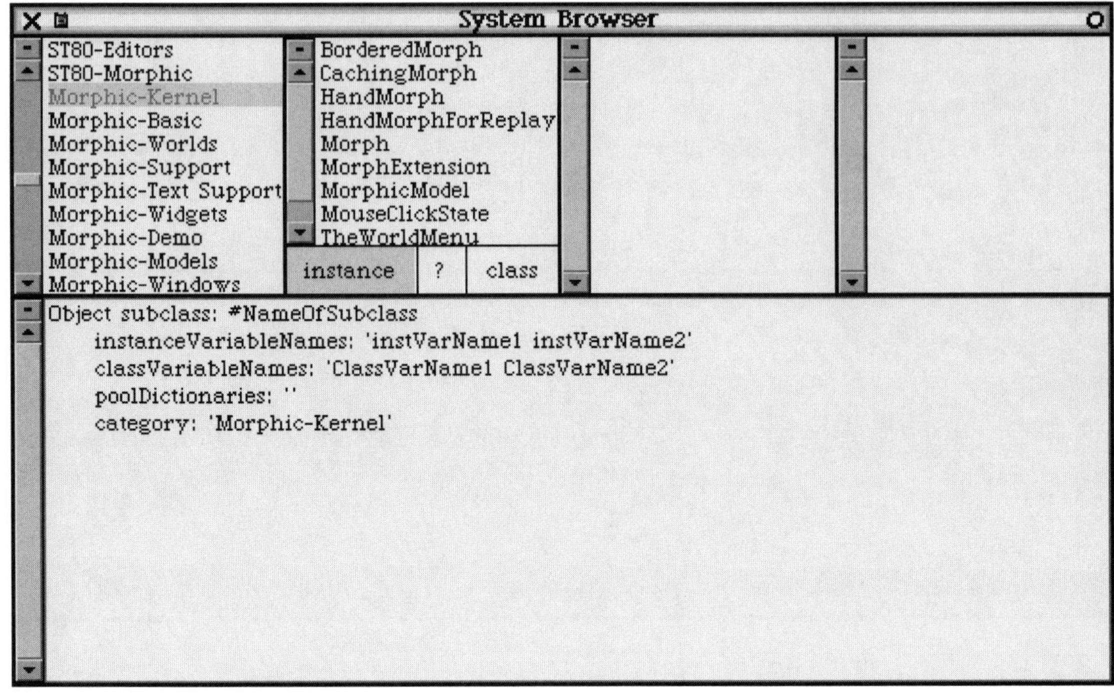

Figure 3–10 Morphic–Kernel category

I see it here, but I'm not sure I understand.

The formerly empty second pane now contains a list of the classes that are part of the **Morphic-Kernel** category. Select the **Morph** class from the second pane. When the Squeak system responds to this action, it'll fill the third pane with a list of method groups. The third pane contains categories, or groups, of related methods. When one of these groups is chosen, the fourth pane will be filled with a list of all of the methods from a particular category. By selecting **—all—**, it's possible to view all of the methods of a class.

Okay, I'm starting to understand how things are organized. What's the stuff in the bottom of the window?

Each time that you make a selection in one of the small, upper panes, specific information is displayed in the lower,

JIM | OBJECTIVE LIBRARIAN

text-editing pane. For example, after **Morphic-Kernel** is selected in the first pane, a generic template for a class is provided. When you create your own classes, you can use this outline as a starting point.

In the case of the second pane, if you select the **Morph** class, the same type of template that you saw previously is shown in the lower pane. However, in this instance, the information is specific to the **Morph** class. Try it out for yourself.

And the third pane?

The pattern of generic to specific is repeated when you make a selection in the third pane. Since the third pane displays general categories of methods, the lower pane displays a generic template for a method.

When you make a selection in the fourth pane, you'll be choosing a single, specific method from either a group of related methods or all of the methods for a particular class. The Smalltalk code that implements the method will be shown in the lower pane. In this instance, try choosing a variety of different methods.

This little experiment has shown me a lot.

Can we work with classes a bit more?

As you learn to program in Smalltalk, you'll spend a great deal of time investigating the classes that make up the Squeak environment. For instance, perhaps you're interested in finding classes related to the operation of the mouse input device.

If you say so.

In the category pane of a System Browser, do a yellow button click. This action will result in the menu shown in Figure 3–11.

In this menu, select the **find class...** option. You'll be prompted with the dialogue box displayed in Figure 3–12. Type the name of the class (or a fragment of the class name)

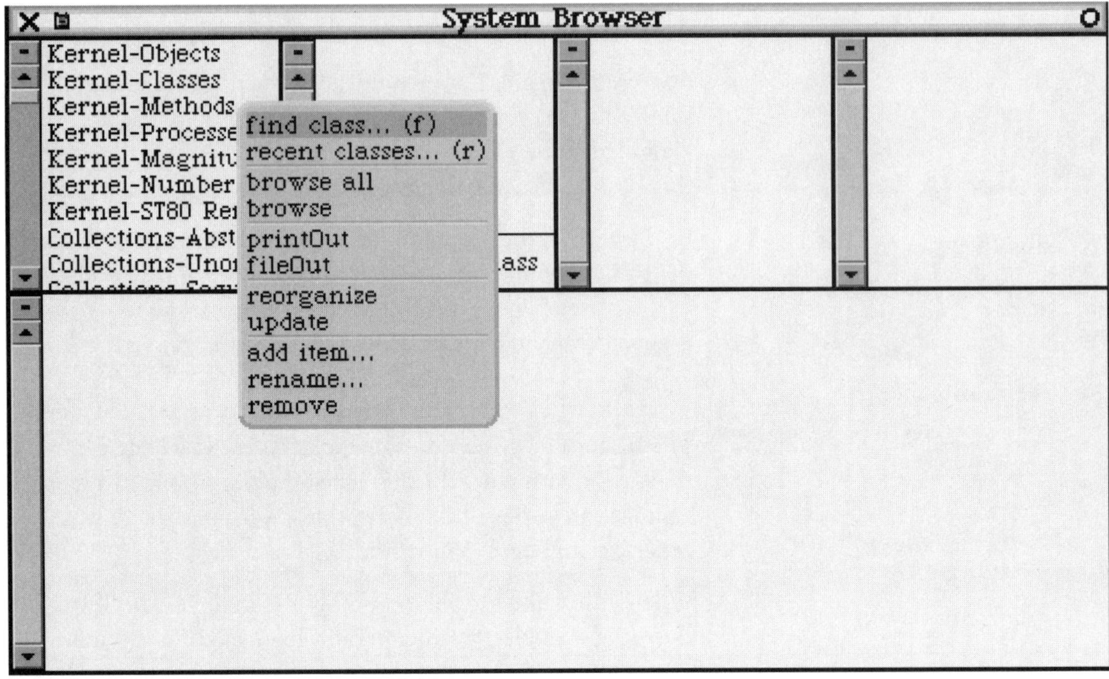

Figure 3–11 The find class... menu option

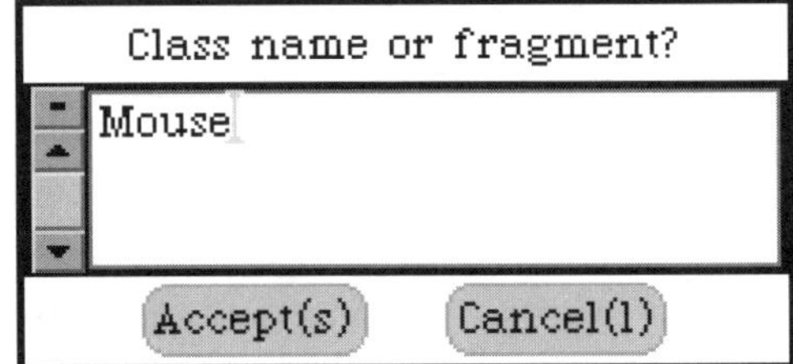

Figure 3–12 Class name or fragment? dialog

that is the intended target of your search. In this case, you should type **Mouse** at the cursor prompt.

Okay, now I've got some kind of mouse menu.

Yes, exactly. As a result of your search request, a Morphic menu will be displayed that contains the names of all of the Squeak classes that contain the string "Mouse," as shown in Figure 3–13. In this instance, the Squeak system doesn't contain a class named Mouse.

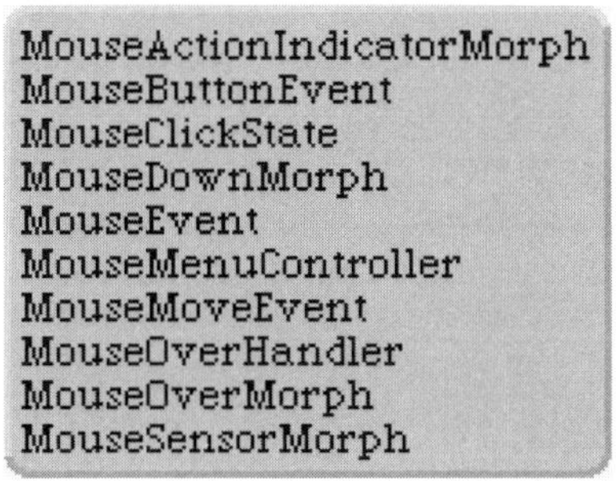

MouseActionIndicatorMorph
MouseButtonEvent
MouseClickState
MouseDownMorph
MouseEvent
MouseMenuController
MouseMoveEvent
MouseOverHandler
MouseOverMorph
MouseSensorMorph

Figure 3–13 Results of search for Mouse

However, Squeak does have numerous classes that contain the string Mouse as a fragment of their full names. You should red-button select one of the class names and watch the result. The class that you select will be shown in the System Browser.

Interesting.

So, I've found a class. What about finding a method?

Ah, Jim, that's just the sort of question I'd hoped you would ask. As you've intuited, the names of classes are not the only things of interest that can be discovered by means of the Squeak system tools. A great deal of useful information concerning the environment can be garnered if you're aware of how to use the tools that Squeak provides.

One such tool is the **Method Finder**. You can open it by selecting the **method finder** choice on the Morphic open menu. Note that its lower pane contains instructions for its use.

Yes, instructions right there in the pane are just the sort of thing I like.

You can experiment with this tool by entering the name, or a fragment of the name, of any method in the upper left pane. In the example shown in Figure 3–14, I entered the string "handler." A list of all of the Squeak method names that contain the string "handler" is displayed in the middle left pane.

Terrific, now I know how to find a class or a method.

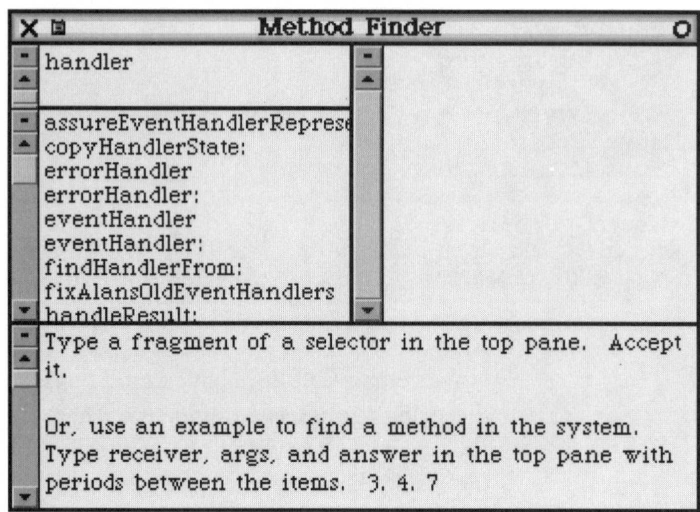

Figure 3–14 Method Finder browser

But what about something that's not there to be found? What about making something new?

Yes, you'll want to extend the functionality of the Squeak system by adding your own classes. In order to demonstrate the mechanics of this process, you are going to go through the steps of creating a new class and adding it to the system. Don't worry about the functionality of this class. We just want to provide an example to follow.

Before you add a new class, you need to create a category to hold that class. Go ahead and open a new System Browser. Make sure that you have not selected any of the items listed in the category pane. If you have, when you add the new category, it'll be displayed as the category item prior to the one that was selected. As long as you don't have any other categories selected, the new one will be added to the end of the list.

In the category pane of a System Browser, do a yellow-button click. This action will result in the same menu that you saw earlier when you were trying to find a class. This time, select the **add item...** menu item, as shown in Figure 3–15.

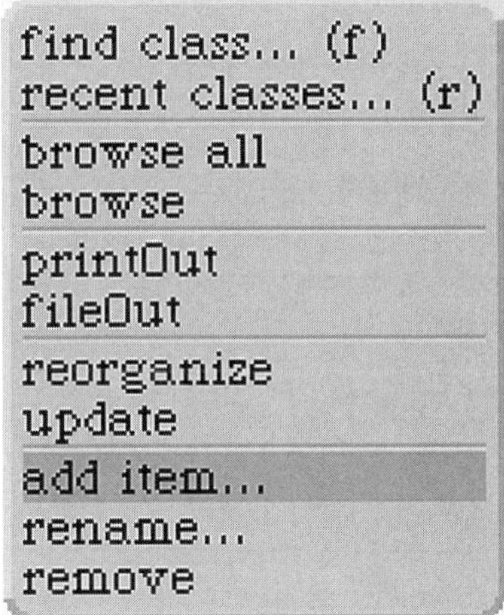

Figure 3–15 The add item... menu option

As a result, a dialogue will prompt you for a new category name.

Yes. What should I enter for the name?

You should enter **ObjectLand** for the new category name. Figure 3–16 shows what you should expect to see.

You can place all of the classes that you create while reading this book into the ObjectLand category.

Great. Is there anything else I need to know about the category that I've so deftly created?

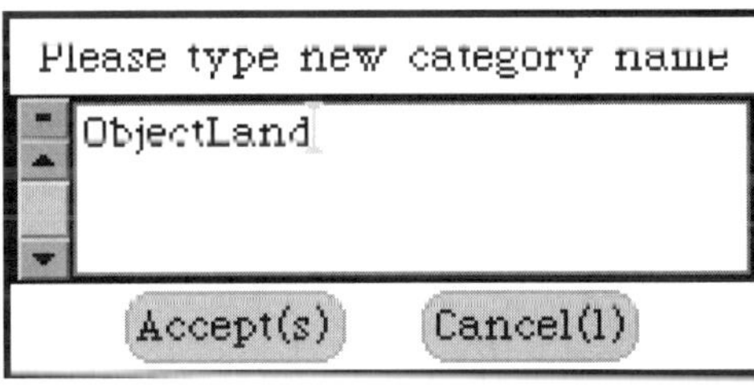

Figure 3–16 The new category dialog

JIM	OBJECTIVE LIBRARIAN
	Well, keep in mind that, before you added a new category, the text editor pane of the System Browser was empty. Now that you've added the ObjectLand category, the text editor pane is displaying a template that you can modify to create a new class. The template is highlighted in the image shown in Figure 3–17.
Okay, I see that. Now what?	
	The first line of Smalltalk code reads as follows:

```
Object subclass: #NameOfClass
```

Replace `NameOfClass` with `Foo`. The second line of the template contains the following code:

```
instanceVariableNames: 'instVarName1
          instVarName2'
```

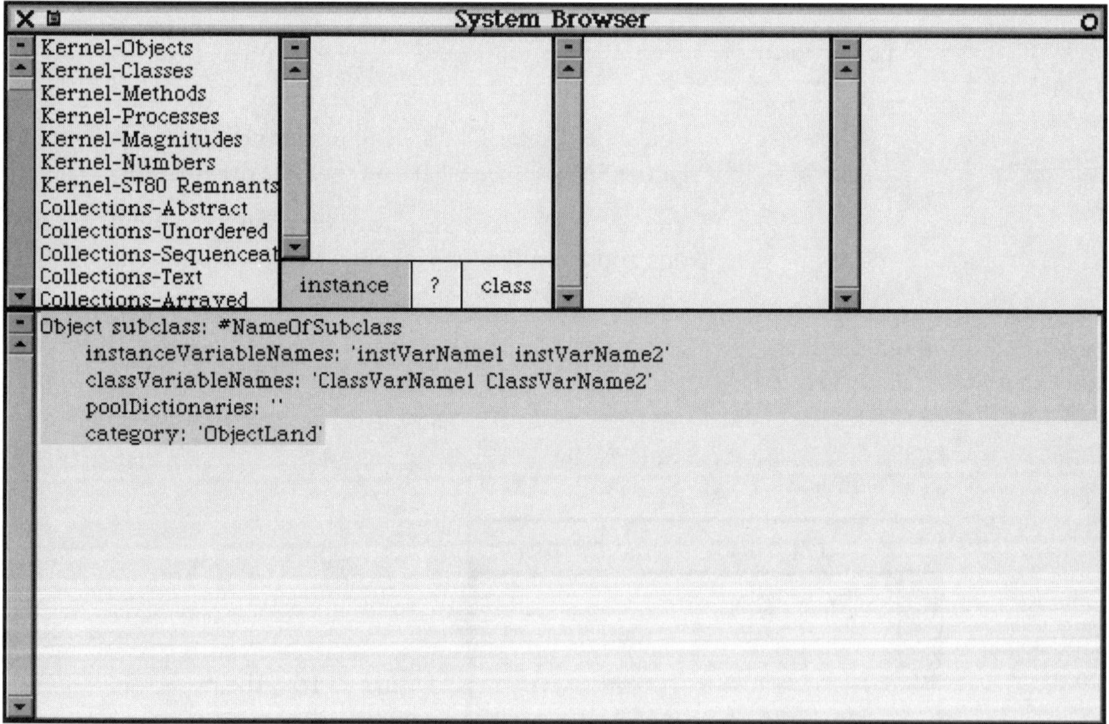

Figure 3–17 System Browser with highlighted class template

JIM	OBJECTIVE LIBRARIAN
	You need to delete `instVarName1` and `instVarName2` while taking care not to remove the single quote characters.
Okay, okay, hold on just a minute.	
	Take it as slowly as you need to, Jim. Just change one thing at a time. When you're ready, do the same thing for the third line of the template, this time removing `ClassVarName1` and `ClassVarName2`. When you're finished, the text editor pane should look like the one in the System Browser displayed in Figure 3–18.
Yes, I've got it.	
	Good. Now, highlight all of the text in the lower pane and do a yellow-button select. In the resulting menu, click on

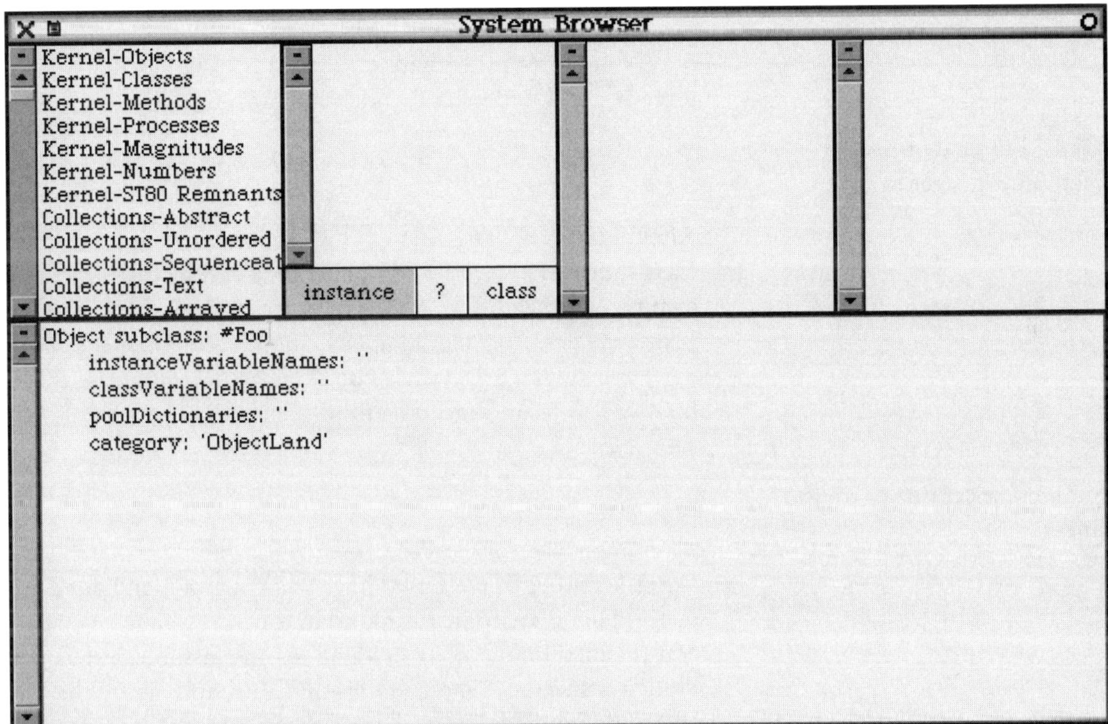

Figure 3–18 Foo class shown in System Browser

JIM | OBJECTIVE LIBRARIAN

accept (**s**). You can test your work by creating an instance of class **Foo**. Open a Workspace and enter the following line of Smalltalk code:

```
MyFoo := Foo new.
```

Highlight the line of code and do a **print it** (**p**). A small, highlighted area containing the text string "`a Foo`" will appear immediately following the line of code. This object is the one being returned as the result of executing the Smalltalk code.

So, I've created a new class?

Yes, Jim, you've created a new class. Are you ready to add a method?

As soon as I grab an espresso. I need a little break while I think about all this.

Sure, I understand. Perhaps you've had enough caffeine already, but I understand your need for a rest.

Okay, I'm ready to add a method. Let's get to it.

After creating a class, the next logical task is to give the new class some behavior by adding methods to the class. Once again, you'll be able to do this by interacting with the System Browser. Class Foo should appear in the second panel of the System Browser. Select class Foo. This action will cause two lines of text to appear in the third panel: "`—all—`" and "`no messages`."

Should I select one of these lines?

Selecting either of these two lines will cause a highlighted method template to be displayed in the lower panel. You can edit the method template in a line-by-line fashion, just as you did with the class template. Or you can simply delete the entire highlighted area and enter the new method directly. In either case, after you are done, your lower panel should contain the Smalltalk method shown in Figure 3–19.

```
sayHelloFoo
    ↑'Hello Foo!'
```

Figure 3–19 Highlighted sayHelloFoo method

Okay, now what's happening?

Since this method is likely to be the first method that you have entered into the Squeak environment, you'll be greeted by the dialogue displayed in Figure 3–20, for which you enter your initials.

And then I accept this?

Yes, after you enter your own initials and click **Accept(s)**, the Squeak environment will track your method additions via your initials.

How do I know it's worked?

Just as you did after you added class **Foo**, you can test your work in a Workspace. Type the following in your Workspace:

```
MyFoo sayHelloFoo.
```

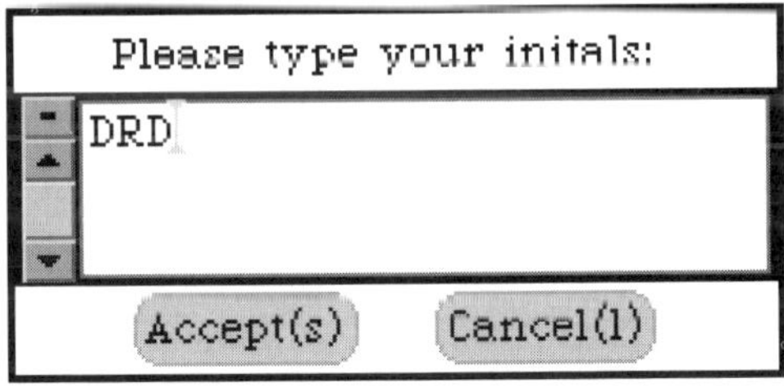

Figure 3–20 Please type your initials dialog

JIM	OBJECTIVE LIBRARIAN
	What did you get for a result?
I got `'Hello Foo!'`—is that right?	
	Great, Jim, that's correct. Let's go on. You need to learn to open a file, and I think you're ready for that, now that you've created a category and added a method.
For you I was born ready. So, yes, how do I open a file?	
	There are two functionally equivalent ways of opening and viewing files in Squeak. Both methods are available from the Morphic **open...** menu. The **file list** and **file...** menu choices are located approximately halfway down the list of choices on the menu. The first method that you will see makes use of the **file...** menu choice.
So, I select **file...**?	
	Yes. After you select **file...**, a menu dialogue entitled **Select a File:** will be opened. As you can see in Figure 3–21, the resulting menu is divided into sections. The topmost section allows you to navigate the file system hierarchy. The middle section displays the subdirectories of the current directory. Finally, the bottom section displays files that are present in the current directory. You should remember that this example is particular to a specific Squeak installation. When you do this on your own, your dialogue will, in all likelihood, not resemble this one.
What do you mean, it won't resemble this one?	
	The items in your directory will be different than the items in my directory, but you'll still have the same kind of menu. Try to experiment a bit with the **Select a File:** menu: navigate the directory structure, open files, and observe what happens.
Hey, when I select a file to view, a file browser displaying the file is started for me.	

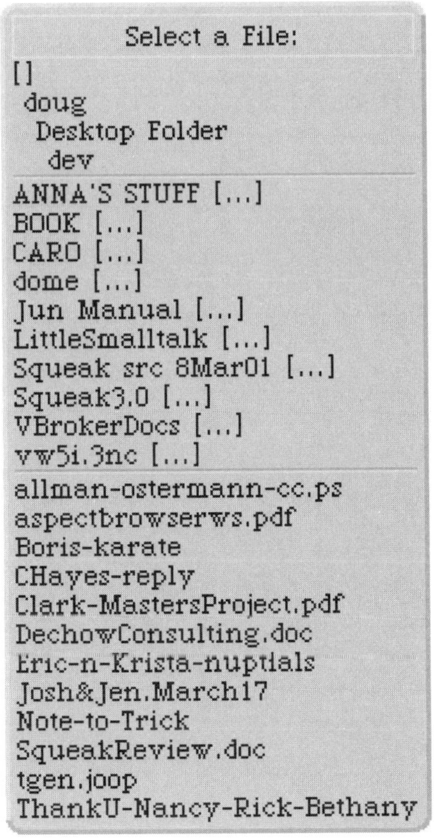

```
Select a File:
[]
 doug
  Desktop Folder
   dev
ANNA'S STUFF [...]
BOOK [...]
CARO [...]
dome [...]
Jun Manual [...]
LittleSmalltalk [...]
Squeak src 8Mar01 [...]
Squeak3.0 [...]
VBrokerDocs [...]
vw5i.3nc [...]
allman-ostermann-cc.ps
aspectbrowserws.pdf
Boris-karate
CHayes-reply
Clark-MastersProject.pdf
DechowConsulting.doc
Eric-n-Krista-nuptials
Josh&Jen.March17
Note-to-Trick
SqueakReview.doc
tgen.joop
ThankU-Nancy-Rick-Bethany
```

Figure 3–21 Select a File: menu

Yes. And as I have pointed out, you can arrive at the same end results by another means.

Okay, lay it on me.

Again, start from the Morphic **open...** menu. However, this time you should select the **file list** menu option. In this situation, when you ultimately select the file that you would like to view, instead of starting a new file browser, the file is displayed in the lower pane, as shown in Figure 3–22.

You'll see the file list browser again when it's time to demonstrate how to add other programmer's code to your Squeak environment.

So, now you know two ways to open a file in Squeak.

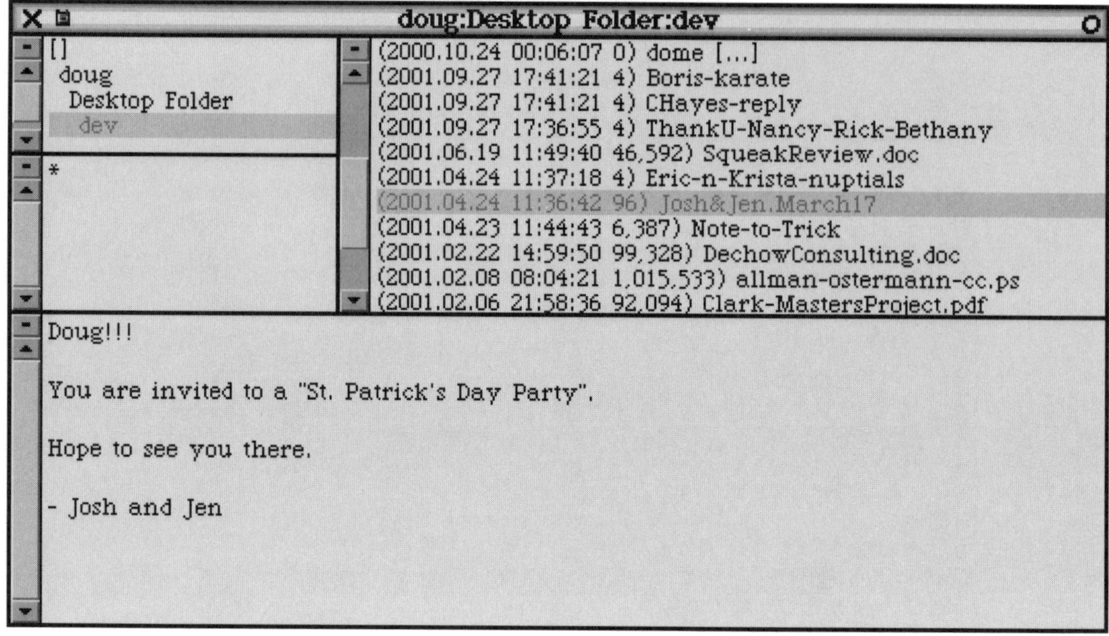

Figure 3–22 File List Browser

I'm finding this visit very helpful.

I thought you would, Jim. Now, you need to understand how to save your work.

Once I learn to save my work, that should wrap things up then?

Not exactly. In fact, there are three more basic tasks you must learn on this trip. But let's start with saving your work.

I should have had that espresso when I had the chance.

Jim, I can sense plenty of enthusiasm.

As with any programming environment, you'll eventually want to be able to save your work. This is certainly accomplished every time that you save the state of the Squeak environment. However, for a variety of reasons, it's also nice to be able to save your work in smaller, more portable pieces.

JIM | OBJECTIVE LIBRARIAN

One way that you can do this in Squeak is to save the individual classes that you create. In the Smalltalk world, this process is referred to as *filing out*. Quite naturally, the result of this process is called a *file out*. To understand this activity better, you should file out the class Foo that you added earlier.

Okay. Go on.

In a System Browser, select the class Foo and yellow-button select the highlighted class name. On the resulting menu, the second grouping of menu choices will contain the **fileOut** item. Select it. As a result, a file named Foo.st will be created. You'll be able to find Foo.st in the same folder or directory as your image and VM files. Foo.st is just an ordinary file containing ASCII text. The Smalltalk code is delimited by exclamation points (!). The contents of Foo.st are as follows:

```
'From Squeak3.0 of 4 February 2001
[latest update: #3545] on 22 March
2001 at 3:35:20 pm'
Object subclass: #Foo
   instanceVariableNames: ''
   classVariableNames: ''
   poolDictionaries: ''
   category: 'ObjectLand'!
!Foo methodsFor: 'greetings' stamp: 'DRD
3/22/2001 23:24'!
sayHelloFoo
   ^'Hello Foo!!'.! !
```

Since you can do a *file out,* can you do a *file in*?

The answer, of course, is yes. You'll see how to file in Smalltalk code in a little while. But that's basically how to save your work.

However, even though you performed a file out of the class, you haven't removed it from the system. You can still test it by creating an instance of Foo and sending it the `sayHelloFoo` message.

Okay, that's good to know.

Jim	Objective Librarian
Can I remove a class or a method from the system?	
	You can certainly remove classes and methods from the environment. However, be forewarned that this activity should only be undertaken with the greatest of care.
I'll keep that in mind.	
	In order to remove an individual method, you need to return, once again, to the System Browser. Select the method to be removed in the fourth pane. In this case, since you have only one method to select—`sayHelloFoo`—the choice is pretty straightforward. You can yellow-button click anywhere in the fourth pane in order to bring up the appropriate menu. Choose the **remove method (x)** item. After the Squeak environment has removed the method, the method's selector will no longer be displayed in the fourth panel.
That was easy!	
	Yes, that's why you must be careful. Don't go removing methods from the environment unless you are sure you want them removed. It's just as easy—and just as dangerous—to remove a class from the Squeak system. In order to complete this experiment, you should go ahead and remove the Foo class from the system. After you've selected the class's name in the second panel, you'll again perform a yellow-button click anywhere in the second pane. Select the **remove class (x)** option from the menu. A dialogue will ask you to confirm that you wish to delete class Foo.
And then it's gone?	
	Just as was done in the case of the method `sayHelloFoo`, the display will be updated to reflect the removal of the class from the system.
Okay, what's left for me to learn on this trip?	
	We're nearly finished. I just want to introduce you to the task of retrieving your own work and the work of others.

JIM

OBJECTIVE LIBRARIAN

Jim: Of course. It's certainly no good to me if I can't retrieve it.

Objective Librarian: Exactly. Earlier, you briefly had the opportunity to examine the file list browser. You're going to revisit the file list browser in order to perform a file in. Filing in Smalltalk code is one of the ways that programmers can add the work of others—and reintroduce their own code—to the Squeak environment.

To see how the process functions, you should file in the class that you just removed—`Foo.st`. After you open a new file list browser, you will see that the file `Foo.st` is one of the files displayed in the upper right pane. When you select this file, its contents will be displayed in the lower pane. You should highlight the entire contents of the file, as shown in Figure 3–23.

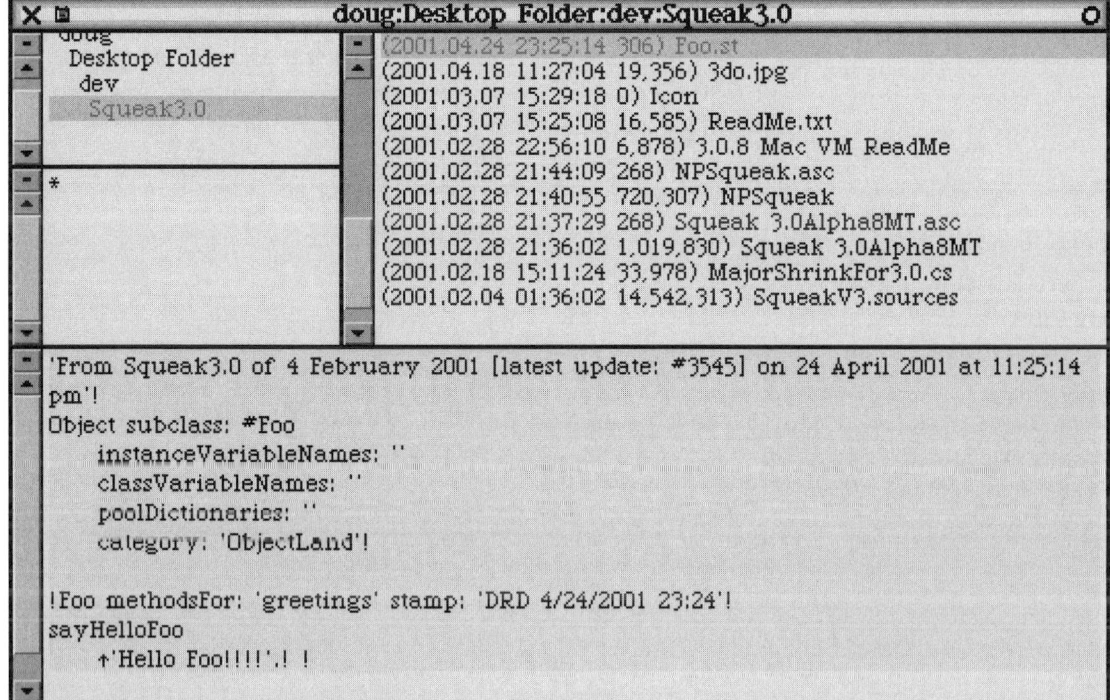

Figure 3–23 Filing in Foo.st

JIM | OBJECTIVE LIBRARIAN

Jim: Yep. And now what?

Objective Librarian: Once you've done this, a yellow-button click will bring up a menu. Choose the **fileIn selection** option. This action will cause the Smalltalk code contained in the file to be loaded into the running Squeak environment.

Jim: What kind of files will I be loading, anyway? You mentioned other people's stuff?

Objective Librarian: Smalltalk programmers have a long history of producing and distributing software known as *goodies*. A goodie is a useful package of Smalltalk code that can be filed into the environment. By learning how to file in code, you'll be able to add goodies to your own Squeak environment.

Jim: Terrific. Is that it, then?

Objective Librarian: Yes, Jim, we're finished for now. This trip has provided you with some very important information you'll need as a Squeak programmer. Feel free to refer back to this visit as you continue to work in the environment. It's been great to see you again, and, sadly, my hope is that you won't need another visit.

Jim: Part of me is sad to go, but I must admit that I need a break. I appreciate your help, Objective Librarian.

Objective Librarian: Have a swell time back in ObjectLand. I'll get back to my organization of reference texts on human oddities.

Jim: Sounds like you won't miss me. I'm off to put all this knowledge to good use.

Summary

New Terms

Morphic Halo	Morphic Handles
System Browser	File List Browser
Goodies	

What Did You Learn?

- How to customize the environment's appearance.
- The benefits of Squeak's Morphic interface, particularly regarding the halo of icons.
- How to use the System Browser.
- How to find a class or a method.
- How to create a class.
- How to add a method.
- How to open a file.
- How to save a file and file out.
- How to remove a class or a method.
- How to retrieve work

Words of Wisdom

You can make Squeak your own by customizing your environment's appearance and also by creating classes, adding methods, and making use of other people's goodies. Spend some time experimenting with the appearance and with saving your own work so that you feel comfortable in a personalized Squeak environment. Make it your own!

What you've learned in this chapter will be useful again and again. With practice, tasks such as opening a file and creating a class will require little effort. However, until you are comfortable performing the basic tasks, remember that this chapter serves as a handy reference.

Be careful not to remove classes and methods unless you are certain they should be removed.

To Do List

In this chapter, you changed the behavior of the scrollbars via the **Preferences** windows. Return to the **Preferences** window and examine the options that are presented for further customizing your environment.

Practice using the System Browser to create classes by adding more methods to class `Foo`.

Bring up a **World** menu. Select the **keep this menu up** item. Blue-button click on the menu to activate its halo. Experiment with manipulating the menu morph by testing each of its handles.

In the preceding chapter, you "designed"—abstractly—a pen object and a paper object in order to understand ways of thinking in the terms of the Smalltalk programming language and the Squeak environment. In other words, in thinking about a pen and a piece of paper, you conceptualized classes, variables (state), and methods (behavior). In this chapter, you were introduced to the tools used to create classes and add methods. Now, combine your understanding of concepts with your knowledge of tools to create a class `Pen` and a class `Paper`.

Part II

Programming in ObjectLand

4

Smalltalk: The Language

Contents at: 'Chapter 4'

#(

messages + message syntax
  unary - binary - keyword
  order of execution
    left to right
    parentheses
    unary
    binary
    keyword
    assignment
    return (^)

numbers + syntax
strings + syntax
characters + syntax
blocks + syntax
arrays + syntax
comments + syntax
additional syntax

variables
  instance
  class
  pool dictionaries
  local variables
  message arguments
  global).

Questions of Interest

- How do I define a class?
- How can I create an instance?
- How do I write a method?

Introduction

In earlier chapters, you took a quick trip to ObjectLand and gained an understanding of the object-oriented programming paradigm. You learned a little about how to think in terms of objects as computational entities and a little about how to design software from objects and messages. Later, we will discuss object-oriented thinking and design in much more detail. For the moment, you must learn more about the syntactical components of Smalltalk so that we can begin to express our object-oriented thoughts in terms of object-oriented implementations.

There is a distinct separation in Squeak between the capabilities of the Smalltalk language, which is very simple and compact, and the capabilities of Squeak's class hierarchy, which is much more extensive. You will focus first on learning the language, because it is the doorway into reading, understanding, and modification of the class hierarchy. Subsequent chapters will be devoted to exploring and understanding the Squeak class hierarchy.

Goals for This Chapter

- To write Smalltalk code and to learn the rules of the compiler.
- To write a little Smalltalk code and to gain an understanding of *compile-time* and *runtime* error messages. The most important concepts that you must carry away from this chapter are as follows:

  The syntax of the language.
  The order of evaluation of messages.
  The scoping and use of variables.

Jim | **Objective Wizard**

Jim: Hey, Wiz! It's been a while. I've been message passing with the Objective Librarian, if you know what I mean.

Objective Wizard: Interaction with the Objective Librarian is essential to your progress.

Jim: Would you go over the basic concepts for me?

Objective Wizard: Sure!

An *object* is a computational entity that contains personal data in the form of variables, and behavior in the form of methods. We can think of two kinds of objects: class and instance. Every instance belongs to exactly one class.

An *instance object* contains personal data in the form of instance variables, and behavior in the form of instance methods. A *class* contains data in the form of class variables, and behavior in the form of class methods. While an instance has its variables all to itself, a class must share its variables with all of its instances.

Pool variables work in much the same way as class variables because they are defined at the class level and are accessible by all of a class's instances. They are different in that several classes can access the same set of pool variables at the same time. Pool variables are used for boring things such as storing character constants, and we will not be talking about them very much.

Jim: Hey! What about messages? Don't they belong in here somewhere?

Objective Wizard: They certainly do. *Messages* are how objects communicate with one another. A message is sent from one object, the sender object, to another, the receiver object, where it activates a method. The method executes, doing some amount of work, and then returns an object to the sender.

JIM	OBJECTIVE WIZARD
You know, that sounds a lot like a function call.	
	In some ways it is, but in others it is not. It is really best to forget about such comparisons and open yourself to learning new material without prior associations.
I'll try. I think I understand all that stuff now. How about the syntax of this language?	
	Fine. First let us discuss the syntax associated with objects, because it is easy. Class objects are referred to by class names. A class name begins with a capital letter. Instance objects do not have names but can be accessed in three ways: 1. the `self` pseudo variable 2. the returned object in an expression 3. a variable or argument
I'm afraid to ask, but what is a pseudo variable?	
	A *pseudo variable* is a variable whose value is assigned by the system.
How is `self` accessed?	
	`self`, in particular, is always the receiver object. To be more exact, `self` is the object that received the message that activated the method that is currently executing. To access `self`, just treat it as if it were an argument to the method.
That's easy. What's next?	
	Messages and message syntax are next. Recall that messages have names called "message selectors." Some messages even have one or more arguments that they carry along with them when they are sent to an object.

JIM | OBJECTIVE WIZARD

If some messages have arguments and others don't, how does that change the syntax of the message?

There are different kinds of messages. Actually, there are three message forms, as follows:

Message Form	Arguments
unary	none
binary	one
keyword	one or more

Would you tell me about unary messages?

Unary messages are simply messages with no arguments. They are common in the existing system, and you, as a designer/implementor, will add many more. A unary message always begins with a lowercase letter.

What are unary messages used for?

Whenever you want to send a message to an object and do not need to carry an argument along with the message, use a unary message.

Please show me examples of unary messages.

Messages without objects have no meaning, so I will send example messages to example objects.

Expression	Returned Object
`'Squeak' size`	`6`
`Pen new`	`a Pen`
`Bag new`	`a Bag()`
`1234 even`	`true`
`Time now`	`8:18:32pm`

Read the code above. In all cases, the object is the first thing in the expression, and the message is the second. If your

JIM	OBJECTIVE WIZARD
	machine is running, type each expression into a Workspace and evaluate it with a **print it**. A printed version of the returned object will be displayed on the screen.
Can you tell me about binary messages?	
	Binary messages are messages with one and only one argument and a special syntax consideration. A binary message selector consists of one or two special characters (where "special" indicates a character other than digits and letters).
What are they used for?	
	They are used primarily for arithmetic and comparison, but they can be used anywhere that you, as a programmer, want to use them.
Please give me some examples.	
	Okay. I will use arithmetic examples in all cases but one. The one nonarithmetic example is the `,` (comma) message, which is used to concatenate objects.

Expression	Returned Object
`3 + 4`	`7`
`61//20`	`3`
`10 < 20`	`true`
`'Squ','eak'`	`'Squeak'`
`#(1 2) , #(3 4)`	`(1 2 3 4)`

JIM	OBJECTIVE WIZARD
	Read the code above. In all cases, the receiver object is the first item in the expression, the message is the second, and the argument is the third. If your machine is running, type each expression into a Workspace and evaluate it with a **print it**. A printed version of the returned object will be shown on the screen.
Tell me about keyword messages.	
	Keyword messages are messages with one or more arguments. A keyword message selector always starts with a lowercase letter and is made up of pieces called *keywords*. Each keyword starts

JIM	OBJECTIVE WIZARD
	with a letter and ends with a : (colon). There is one keyword for each argument. Look at the examples, and you will understand.
What are they used for?	
	They can be used for any message send that requires one or more arguments. With the exception of arithmetic and comparison, keyword messages normally are used when one or more arguments need to be passed with the message send.
How about some examples of keyword messages?	
	That is no problem. Each of the following expressions includes just one keyword message send.

Expression	Returned Object

`Smalltalk`
`   at: #Pi`
`   put: 3.14.`
	`3.14`

`Array new: 2.`	`#(nil nil)`

`50`
`   between: 10`
`   and: 90.`
	`true`

`Bag new add: 'Stuff'.`	`'Stuff'`

JIM	OBJECTIVE WIZARD
	Read the code above. Whereas the receiver object is always the first thing in the expression, the keywords of the message selector and the arguments alternate. If your machine is running, type each expression into a Workspace and evaluate it with a **print it**. A printed version of the returned object will be displayed on the screen.
Are there any other message forms?	
	No—well, there is one other, but it is not really a message form. It is actually more of a programmer's convenience. It is a way of cascading messages and is usually called a *cascade message*. The additional syntax for the cascade is the ; (semicolon). The cascade protocol allows multiple message sends to the same object. Look at the following examples.

JIM | OBJECTIVE WIZARD

Example without cascade:

```
MyPen := Pen new.
MyPen up.
MyPen color: Color black.
MyPen goto: 10@10.
MyPen turn: 90.
MyPen down.
MyPen go: 100.
```

Same example with cascade:

```
MyPen := Pen new.
   up;
   black;
   goto: 10@10;
   turn: 90;
   down;
   go: 100;
   yourself.
```

In the first example, we create an instance of class `Pen` by sending the `new` message to the class `Pen` and assigning the instance that is created to the global variable `MyPen`. We then start sending individual messages to `MyPen` to get it to do penlike things. Note that we have to state explicitly the object (`MyPen`) to which each message is sent. Note also that there is a `.` (period) at the end of each line. The period is the statement terminator, which means that each line in this chunk of code is an individual statement.

In the second example, using the cascade protocol, we accomplish the same task by placing a `;` (semicolon) after each message. The semicolon tells Squeak to send the next message to the same object to which the previous message was sent.

The `yourself` message is usually included as the last message send in a cascade because it forces a return of the receiving object. The message `yourself` always returns `self`. This is considered good programming style because it guarantees control over what is returned from the cascaded series of message sends.

JIM	OBJECTIVE WIZARD
I'm a little confused by this returned value stuff.	
	Remember that every message send returns an object. In the case of cascaded messages, the object returned is whatever the last message send returns. When you include the `yourself` message as the final message, you ensure that the receiving object, `self`, will be returned from the expression. Because cascades are used to do multiple operations to a single object, returning that object is usually desired.
When do I use cascade messages?	
	Use cascade messages whenever you want to send several separate messages to the same object. It is used quite often in pen drawing code.
What is a statement in Smalltalk?	
	A *statement* is one or more message sends terminated by a period. The period is optional at the end of the last statement in a method.
Can a statement have more than one message send in it?	
	Sure.
How about some examples of complex statements?	
	Later. By the way, the words *statement* and *expression* mean the same thing in Smalltalk.
How does Smalltalk decide which messages get sent in what order?	
	There are rules for the order of execution.
What is that order of execution?	

JIM	OBJECTIVE WIZARD

Expressions are executed in the following order:

1. code in parentheses
2. unary message sends (left to right)
3. binary message sends (left to right)
4. keyword message sends
5. assignments
6. returns

JIM: Show me an example.

```
Price := 87.0 + (12.00 * 3) + 5000 / 50.
```

This expression would be executed in the following order:

Code	Returned Object
12.00 * 3	36.0
87.0 + 36.0	123.0
123.0 + 5000	5123.0
5123.0 / 50	102.46
Price := 102.46	102.46

JIM: Would you read this code for me?

Yes! I am happy that you asked, because code reading is one of the most important skills you need to learn. Actually, you should make a habit of reading all Smalltalk code that you view. I will give you an example of what Smalltalk code reading sounds like.

Send the binary message `*` to the instance of class `Float` `12.00`, with the instance of class `Integer` `3` as an argument. The instance of class `Float` `36.0` is returned from this message send.

Send the binary message `+` to the instance of class `Float` `87.0`, with the instance of class `Float` created by the last message send as the argument. Return the instance of class `Float` `123.0`.

JIM | OBJECTIVE WIZARD

Send the binary message + to the instance of class Float 123.0, with the instance of class Integer 5000 as the argument. Return the instance of class Float 5123.0.

Send the binary message / to the instance of class Float returned from the last message send, with the instance of class Integer 50 as the argument. Return the instance of class Float 102.46.

Finally, assign the instance of class Float 102.46 to the global variable Price. Price is now 102.46, which is an instance of class Float.

Would you do that again with some different code?

Yes. Consider the following piece of code:

```
#(1 2 3 3 45 43 43 99 10 12 3 7)
   asSet
      asSortedCollection
            asArray.
```

This code sends the unary message asSet to the instance of Array #(1 2 3 3 45 43 43 99 10 12 3 7), which answers an object that is an instance of the class Set. The asSortedCollection message is then sent to the instance of class Set, which was answered from the asSet message send. The asSortedCollection message answers an instance of the class SortedCollection, and the asArray message is sent to that instance. The asArray message answers an instance of the class Array.

The overall effect of this expression is to strip the redundant elements from the original array and answer a new array with all elements sorted in ascending order.

How about doing it one more time with different code?

Sure. Consider the following piece of code:

```
9 factorial
   between: (10 * 10000)
   and: (50 * 10000).
```

JIM	OBJECTIVE WIZARD
	The unary message `factorial` is sent to the integer instance `9`, and the integer instance `362880` is returned. The `between:and:` keyword message is then sent to `362880` with the arguments `(10 * 10000) and (50 * 10000)`. Because these arguments are in parentheses, they are evaluated before the keyword message is evaluated. These evaluations return integer instances of `100000` and `500000`, respectively. The `between:and:` is evaluated, and it is determined that `362880` is between `100000` and `500000`. The overall expression returns `true`.
How can you tell what is a class, instance, message, or variable?	
	You already know the first clue. Everything you read in a Smalltalk expression will be one of the following: class name constant object (number, string, and so on) message selector variable containing an object punctuation (that is, ^, :=, ; , " , # , ., and so on) Every word you read in an expression is one of these five constructs. The second clue to reading Smalltalk code is to look at the first letter of the word you are trying to understand. If it begins with a capital letter, then it is one of the following: class name global variable referencing an object class variable pool variable If it is a class name, then look in the System Browser to find out more about it. If it is a global variable, then you can send an **`inspect`** message to it. You should remember the

JIM | OBJECTIVE WIZARD

role of inspectors from your visit with the Objective Librarian.

If it begins with a lowercase letter, then it is one of the following:

local variable referencing an object

argument referencing an object

instance variable referencing an object

message

If it is a local variable or argument, it will be declared somewhere in the method code you are reading. If it is an instance variable, it will be a part of the object's class definition. Look at the definition of the object's class using the System Browser. If it is none of the above, it is a message.

What global variables are available?

There are many global variables already in the Squeak system. You can examine all of the global variables by using the following piece of code:

```
(Smalltalk reject: [:value |
      value isKindOf: Behavior])
   inspect.
```

If you want to add a new variable, the easiest way is just to use it. The system will ask you if you want to make the new variable a global variable; answer yes, and you're all set. You can explicitly add new global variables by using a piece of code like this:

```
Smalltalk at: #MyVariable put: nil.
```

You may have noticed "Smalltalk" in both of these pieces of code. Smalltalk, in these pieces of code, refers to an object that keeps track of all the global variables. If you want to see *all* of the global variables, including the class names, you can use the following code:

```
Smalltalk inspect.
```

JIM

OBJECTIVE WIZARD

What does the syntax of the language look like?

I have positioned a summary of the Smalltalk syntax at the end of our current discussion here, before the To Do List. Look it over; study it a bit. The best way to learn syntax is to use it, and you will be using it soon.

Do any objects use a special syntax?

Yes, instances of `Array`, `Character`, `String`, and `Symbol` use special syntax. Another kind of object, called a block, also has a special syntax. Let us examine them one at a time.

Arrays can be created by using a # (hash mark) followed by `(` (begin parenthesis) followed by some number of elements. The end of the array is marked with `)` (end parenthesis). Arrays built in this way can contain only strings, symbols, characters, and other arrays. Here are some examples:

```
#(1 2 47.9)
#($a 'Hi There')
#(ABC ($a $b $c))
```

Notice that the last array listed contains two elements. The first is a symbol, and the second is an array. Note that the # (hash mark) is skipped for special syntax used inside the array.

A *character* is an object that can be referenced by preceding it with a dollar sign. For example, `$a` is the lowercase letter *a*, `$3` is the character `3`, and `$$` is the character `$`.

Strings are easily recognizable. Any sequence of characters enclosed in single quotes is a Smalltalk string. Here is an example:

```
'Hello there'
'1 2 3 4'
'Squeak inspect'
```

Symbols are sequences of characters, just like strings; the only difference is that, when two symbols are created with the same sequence of characters, they are always the same object. (This special property is not one you need to worry

JIM | OBJECTIVE WIZARD

about now, but it is important for the way in which several parts of the Squeak system work.) A symbol is normally a single line with no spaces, starting with a letter, and it is preceded by a # (hash mark). Here are some examples:

```
#A
#between:and:
#name
```

Blocks are chunks of code packaged as objects. We will discuss them in much more detail later on. The syntax for a block is simply square brackets around some code. Other kinds of blocks have one or two arguments before the code. The arguments are preceded by a : (colon) and followed by an | (upright line). Here are some examples of blocks:

```
[:number | 10 * number - 1]
[:a :b | a raisedTo: b]
```

What about variables?

Variables refer to objects. If you are a variable, your issues of interest are

1. duration of your existence
2. scope of influence
3. capitalization
4. your value (which is always an object)

What about scope and usage of variables?

The kinds of variables available to Squeak programmers are instance, class, pool, local, and global.

Instance, class, and pool variables are included as part of the class definition. Local variables, including arguments, are defined within each method. Global variables are defined for the entire system by adding them to the `Squeak` system dictionary.

Although it is added to the class definition, each instance gets its own set of instance variables. The values assigned to

JIM | OBJECTIVE WIZARD

the instance variables differentiate various instances of the same class. Instance variables for a particular object can be accessed only by methods activated when that object receives a message.

Class variables are used to describe information associated with an entire class. The class and all its instances have access to a class variable.

Global variables are available anywhere in the environment. They exist until they are intentionally removed. Here is the code that is used to add a new global variable:

```
Smalltalk at: #MyGlobal put: nil.
```

To remove one, use the following code:

```
Smalltalk removeKey: #MyGlobal.
```

Pool variables are grouped into pool dictionaries. A class definition can access the entire pool of variables by adding the name of the pool dictionary to its class definition. Pool variables normally are used only to ease reference to constant values.

Local variables are available only in the method in which they are declared. A local variable is created when the method starts executing and exists until that method returns. Local variables include method arguments and block arguments. Block arguments should be treated as if they are valid only between the square brackets that define the block.

Global, class, and pool variables should always start with a capital letter. Instance and local variables always begin with a lowercase letter.

Is that all?

No, there are also five items of interest called *pseudo variables*: `nil`, `true`, `false`, `self`, and `super`. Pseudo variables are different in that they cannot be assigned, and, in the cases of `nil`, `true`, and `false`, their values are always the same.

JIM | OBJECTIVE WIZARD

The pseudo variables `nil`, `true`, and `false` are instances of the following classes:

Class	Instance
UndefinedObject	nil
True	true
False	false

The pseudo variable `self`, as I have mentioned before, always refers to the receiver object. The pseudo variable `super` is just like `self`, but with a twist. It refers to the receiver object, but when a message is sent to it, it begins to look for the method to execute starting in its superclasses method list. This is done to improve code reusability when using inheritance, which I will discuss later.

I'm pretty sure I understand the different kinds of variables, but how do I set their values?

Oh, pardon me. I should have mentioned that assignment is done using the := (colon and equal sign) operator. Although it looks like a binary message send, it is actually a special operation. You may recall that, in the order of execution, an assignment was almost at the end of the list. Here are some code examples of assignment:

```
Birthday := '2 Jan 1983' asDate.
total := x + y + z.
count := count + 1.
aString := 'Happy Birthday'.
```

The Squeak version of Smalltalk also allows assignment using a special left-arrow character that is mapped to the underscore key on your keyboard. I should also mention that the return operation, which is a ^ (caret) preceding an expression, answers the value to return from the method.

Since every message returns some object as its value, then must every method have a return operation in it?

JIM | OBJECTIVE WIZARD

Not exactly. If you do not put a return operation in a method, a default is used. The default is to return the receiver object.

Now that I think about it, I don't really know how to write a method yet. The Objective Librarian held my hand through this sort of thing earlier, and I appreciated that, but perhaps you could show me how to write a method.

It is not difficult. Let us look at a method and discuss its structure.

```
raisedToInteger: anInteger
   "Answer myself raised to
   the integer power anInteger."

   | answer |
   answer := 1.
   anInteger timesRepeat: [
      answer := answer * self].
   ^answer.
```

The first line in this method is the message selector. It includes the name of the method (`raisedToInteger:`) and declares the argument (`anInteger`). The second and third lines constitute a comment. You can place a comment just about anywhere within the method code, but a comment just below the message pattern is standard. On the fourth line is a local variable declaration for a variable called `answer`. If you are not using any local variables, the upright lines can be eliminated.

The last four lines of the method comprise the actual Smalltalk code. We do not need to talk about what the code actually does, but I should point out that the first line of code is an assignment, and the last line returns a value from the method.

Why does the comment use the word *myself* as if it were a person?

Jim	Objective Wizard
	The word `myself` here simply refers to the receiver object. It is fairly common to write method comments in this manner because it gives the writer an easy way to refer to the receiver object. Writing comments in an anthropomorphic fashion also helps you to think in terms of intelligent objects.
What happens if I make a mistake when adding a method?	
	When you try to save your new or modified method, the compiler will let you know if it does not like something. It does this by inserting a short error message directly into your code. The error message is placed just before the code that the compiler thinks is wrong.
I think I understand, but what does some other code look like, how do I write it, and where does it go? Turn me loose, Wizard. I want to write some Smalltalk code.	
	So I see! I suggest you go to the To Do List positioned just beyond our discussion. Aloha.

Summary

New Terms

Pool Variable

Pool Dictionary

Unary Message

Binary Message

Keyword Message

Statement

Message Pattern

Class Definition

Cascaded Messages

What Did You Learn?

- The three message types and cascaded messages.
- The order of execution.
- How to read Squeak code.
- The special syntax of arrays, characters, strings, and symbols.
- Pseudo variables `true`, `false`, `nil`, `self`, and `super`.
- How a method is put together.

Words of Wisdom

Take some time to learn how to use the **implementors** and **senders** options on the methods menu in the System Browser. They will allow you to trace quickly who sends a message and what it is used for.

When you see Smalltalk code, *look* at it. Read it to yourself, and try to understand what it is doing. This reading practice will improve your comprehension of the system and Squeak programming techniques very quickly. Warning: Don't read the code out loud—people might think you're strange.

Watch your order of execution, particularly when doing numeric expressions. It may not work the way you expect it to. When in doubt, use parentheses.

Syntax Summary

Special Symbols

Symbol	Meaning	Example
:=	assignment operator	`pages := pages + 1.`
.	statement terminator	`A := A reversed.`
;	cascade protocol	
^	return the following object	`^name`
[ ]	block delimiter	`[Smalltalk beep]`
( )	expression delimiter	`salary := 3.47 * (43 + 5)`
:	keyword message	`Contents at: 'Chapter 1'`
" "	comment	`"This is  a comment"`
' '	string	`'This is a string'`
#	symbol or array constant	`#(one 33 house xyz)`
$	character constant	`$k`
		local variables	`| anArray index |`

Scoping of Variables

Variable	Scope
local	single method execution
instance	single instance
class	class and all of its instances
pool	all classes that specify the pool dictionary
global	everywhere

Order of Execution

code in parentheses

unary message sends (left to right)

binary message sends (left to right)

keyword message sends

assignments

returns

To Do List

Your best friend owns a music store, and you have decided to help him implement a sales tracking system. Use the System Browser to add two new classes: `CompactDisc` and `CDTrack`.

CompactDisk should have three instance variables: `title`, `artist`, and `tracks`.

`CDTrack` should have three instance variables: `title`, `trackNumber`, and `length`.

You have another friend who owns a computer store and you have decided to help him, too. Create a class to represent a diskette. Call it `Diskette`. Some of the characteristics you may want to represent are:

Instance Variable	Comment
type	DS, SS, HD, and so on
size	Diameter of disk
capacity	How much storage it has
label	Name of the disk
location	Which box in your closet
lastUsedDate	Last time the disk was used

Instance method	Comment
location	Answer the location of the disk
location:	Set the location to a new location
type	Answer the type of disk
size	Answer the size of the disk
capacity	Answer the capacity of the disk
label	Answer the name of the disk
label:	Change the name of the disk
lastUsed	Answer the last used date
lastUsed:	Update the last used date

Extra credit: Instead of helping your friend who owns a computer store, help your friend who owns a video store or hair salon. Create a class to represent a DVD or hair-color product, make a list of characteristics you want to represent, and delineate instance variables, instance methods, and their respective comments in a chart like the one above.

5

Back to ObjectLand

Contents at: 'Chapter 5'

#(

encapsulation

polymorphism

inheritance
  overriding inheritance
  super

learning the class hierarchy
  finding classes
  categorizing classes
  abstract and concrete classes

using the class hierarchy
  subclassing
  copy/paste
  extensions

expanding the class hierarchy
  adding new classes
  generalizing and specializing
  using inheritance).

Questions of Interest

- When and what do I subclass?
- How can I benefit from inheritance?

- When do I use instance and class variables?
- How about Global and Pool variables?

Introduction

Earlier, you took a quick trip to ObjectLand and gained an understanding of the object-oriented programming paradigm. You learned a little about how to think of objects as computational entities, and a little about how to design software from objects and messages. Much later, you will discuss object-oriented thinking and design in greater detail. In this chapter, you put yourself back in ObjectLand to learn the rest of the story about the object-oriented paradigm.

You find that there are more concepts to learn:

1. encapsulation
2. polymorphism
3. inheritance

You find, too, additional information about how the system uses these capabilities.

You also begin to learn more about the organization of the class hierarchy.

Goals for This Chapter

- To learn about the object-oriented paradigm and to map some small problems into object-oriented representations.
- To learn to use encapsulation, polymorphism, and inheritance in our design and implementation.

JIM	OBJECTIVE WIZARD
I'm back! I love writing code in Smalltalk!	
	Good! Let us get to work! We have been making excellent progress. On this trip, I would like to introduce you to some of the moral fiber of ObjectLand. There are three underlying capabilities that are particularly interesting. We call them encapsulation polymorphism inheritance Let us look at them one at a time.
I'm game.	
What is encapsulation?	
	Encapsulation is a big word used to describe the privacy of an object.
How can I use it?	
	You do not have a choice; it is enforced. Objects are encapsulated by nature, but you can design objects whose role in life is to encapsulate. These objects are called, as you might expect, "encapsulators."
There's no way I can avoid encapsulation?	
	No. As you probably understand in human terms, privacy is very important—but you can choose either to use encapsulation or to try to work around it. Encapsulation is not enforced to make your life difficult, instead, it is a way to keep the inside of an object from getting unexpectedly, and incorrectly, altered.
I think I see. Encapsulation keeps objects from getting trashed by some other object. They keep their original integrity because they are encapsulated.	

JIM	OBJECTIVE WIZARD
	Well put. And by knowing that encapsulation exists and why it is useful, you can write better code.
I don't quite see how encapsulation functions. If the object is private, how can I work with it?	
	An object can be accessed only by sending it a message. If an object's message interface does not include a way to access an instance variable directly, then you have no way to look at or change that variable from outside the object.
So, if I need to access some information that's kept in an instance variable, I write methods that do it.	
	Yes! Very good, Jim. You are learning quickly that you can work with the object's privacy, or encapsulation. Writing these kinds of messages is such a common activity that they have names. A *get* method is one written just to get and answer the value of an instance variable. A *set* method is one written just to set the value of an instance variable.
I see.	
And what is polymorphism?	
	Polymorphism refers literally to the capability to assume different forms. In Smalltalk, polymorphism refers to the ability of a given message to assume different functions, depending on the object that receives the message.
How can a message function differently, depending on what object it is sent to?	
	Keep in mind that the message is a selector. The method is the actual code that results in the functionality. Polymorphism relies on this difference between message and method and the fact that Smalltalk uses dynamic, or late, binding of message to method. In Smalltalk, the binding of a message to the method it will activate occurs when the message is sent. The method to be activated is chosen by the receiving object.

JIM	OBJECTIVE WIZARD
	So, it is really the receiving object that determines exactly what method is executed and, consequently, what function is performed.
How about some examples?	

Sure! Look at the following code:

Expression	Answer
`3 + 4`	`7`
`3.2 + 3.14`	`6.34`
`(10@30) + (10@10)`	`20@40`
`(1/2) + (32/64)`	`1`

Here, the message + is sent to instances of four different classes, as follows: `Integer`, `Float`, `Point`, and `Fraction`. In each case, the method that is activated answers the sum of the receiver and the argument; each summation, however, is done in a different way.

For example, while the sum of two integers is simply a primitive operation with no further Smalltalk code, the sum of two points looks like this code:

```
+ aPoint
      "Answer the sum of myself
       and aPoint."
   ^Point new
      x: (self x + aPoint x)
      y: (self y + aPoint y).
```

So, the + message is polymorphic because it is part of the message interface for several classes, and each class implements it in the way that is most appropriate.

Different object-oriented languages have slightly different implementations of polymorphism, some of which are limited in some way. Smalltalk's polymorphism works all the time for every message send.

How about some more examples?

JIM	OBJECTIVE WIZARD

Sure! Look at the following code:

Expression	Answer
`'ObjectLand' size.`	10
`#(q w e r t y ) size.`	6
`('one', 'two') size.`	6

`Set new`
`   addAll: 'one', 'two';`
`   size.`
	5

Here, the size message is sent to instances of classes `String`, `Array`, and `Set`. Each of these subclasses of `collection` answers the number of elements it contains, but each computes its number of elements in a different way.

Notice that, in all these cases, `size` answers the number of elements in the object to which it was sent, even though the method that computed the size was different. Two objects receiving the same message should behave in a similar way.

How can I use polymorphism in my code?

Well, the first step is to learn the messages that are used polymorphically in the class hierarchy. This learning must be accomplished through experience but can be augmented by selecting a message in a class hierarchy browser and using the **implementors** option in the methods menu. The implementors window will then open to a list of all classes that implement the message you have chosen. If there is only one item in the list, then the message you have chosen is not used by more than one class and, therefore, does not take advantage of polymorphism. If there are many items, then you can see what classes implement the message.

The second step is to design using polymorphism. The robot exercises in the To Do List at the end of this chapter are good examples for designing with polymorphism.

What is the best way to learn more about polymorphism?

JIM	OBJECTIVE WIZARD
	The best way to learn is to do. In your case, you will learn by designing your projects to use polymorphism. It is particularly effective when used with inheritance.
Inheritance?	
	Yes, inheritance, our next topic.

Inheritance is a powerful problem-solving tool available to Squeak programmers. It is conceptually very simple. All Smalltalk classes exist in a class-subclass hierarchy. When you view the class hierarchy using a System Browser, you will notice that some classes in the class list are indented. An indented class is a subclass of the class from which it is indented. Look at the following example:

```
Number
   Float
   Fraction
   Integer
```

In this example, the class `Number` is the superclass of `Float`, `Fraction`, and `Integer`. Conversely, `Float`, `Fraction`, and `Integer` are subclasses of `Number`.

JIM: So, how is this class-subclass relationship useful?

OBJECTIVE WIZARD: Think of inheritance as a problem-solving tool rather than as a concept. If you think of it as a concept, then it becomes something you must learn. If you think of it as a problem-solving tool, then it becomes something you can use. Do you understand the distinction?

JIM: Yes, but I still don't know what's useful about it.

OBJECTIVE WIZARD: In problem solving, it is often useful first to solve a piece of the problem in a general sense and then to solve that piece in a more specific way by filling in the details that specialize the general solution to the specific problem you are trying to solve.

With inheritance, you can solve the general characteristics of the problem in a superclass and create subclasses to implement the specific solutions. The `Number` classes are a good

JIM	OBJECTIVE WIZARD
	example of this approach. (Class `Number` is a very general solution to the problem of what it means to be a number.) Much of the number behavior is implemented in the `Number` class, but the subclasses implement specialized versions of numbers (that is, `Integer`, `Float`, and `Fraction`). When inheritance is used, the subclasses inherit all the variables and methods implemented in the `Number` class and then proceed to add their own variables and methods to become specializations of `Number`.
Wow, and I am reusing much of the code I write in the `Number` class in the subclasses, right?	
	Right!
Just what is inherited?	
	Basically, all the methods and variables of a superclass are available to its subclasses.
How about an example?	
	Gladly. Explore the `Number` hierarchy, and find out which methods used in `Integer` and `Float` operations are actually inherited from `Number` or its superclass `Magnitude`. Also, look for the methods from `Number` that have been overridden in `Float` and `Integer`.
Overriding inheritance? What is that about?	
	At times, you will be working with a subclass and will realize that you are inheriting something that you do not want. If you are inheriting variables that are of no use to your subclass, you can simply ignore them. If this happens often or if there are many variables that you do not wish to inherit, then redesign the superclass-subclass relationship and rebuild the classes. If you are inheriting methods that you wish to use in a different manner in your subclass, then override them by implementing a method with the same message selector in the subclass.

JIM	OBJECTIVE WIZARD
	If you wish to call an overridden method, you can use the super pseudo variable, and the superclass version of the method will be used. The super is used in your code by placing it before the message selector that you are sending.
I don't understand that part about using super to call overridden methods. Could you explain it to me again?	

Of course. The pseudo variable super works just like self, except that it will look only for methods that you inherit. By skipping your class's so-called personal methods, it is able to call a method that has been overridden. This is the *only* reason that super exists.

It is very rare to use super other than within the method that is overriding what you are trying to call. For example, the following method uses the overridden method to do most of its work:

```
initialize
   "Private - Initialize my
    instance variables."
super initialize.
z := 0.
```

This method first calls the method it is overriding and then initializes an extra instance variable.

Jim: How about an example of inheritance?

Objective Wizard: All right, but I want you to do some of the work. Pick an object for us to work with.

Jim: How about a book?

Objective Wizard: That will be fine. We can use the point of view of a librarian trying to keep track of the books in a library.

Jim: Like the Objective Librarian?

Objective Wizard: Yes, I suppose you can think of the Objective Librarian. What things about a book would she want to track, given her somewhat idiosyncratic interests?

JIM | OBJECTIVE WIZARD

Jim: I wish she were here. Let's see…title and author, for sure. Maybe publication date, since she's interested in history and stuff. And probably that number used to reference books.

Objective Wizard: The Dewey decimal or Library of Congress classification. That number is often crucial for librarians. Why don't you choose one type of cataloguing?

Jim: Dewey decimal, definitely.

Objective Wizard: I would like to add the number of pages as well.

Jim: Yes, I always want to know how long a book is.

Objective Wizard: Here is our conceptual definition so far:

Book (Subclass of Object)
    title
    author
    deweyNumber
    pageCount

What is our next step?

Jim: Hmm…earlier you said something about creating general solutions. Is this a good time to do that?

Objective Wizard: A very good time. Because a library is our intended audience, I think a general class called `Document` would be in order.

Jim: Sure, libraries have lots of inventory besides books: magazines, reports, tapes…

Objective Wizard: Good! For this example, let us say that a `Document` has a `title` and a `deweyNumber`. Now, our design looks like this notation:

JIM	OBJECTIVE WIZARD

```
Document (Subclass of Object)
   title
   deweyNumber

Book (Subclass of Document)
   author
   pageCount
```

Note that I included the superclass in parentheses after the class name. You will find such references very important when you start designing.

Jim: I believe I understand inheritance now, but it would help if you ran through all the concepts one more time.

Objective Wizard: I can do that.

Encapsulation protects the instance variables of an object from access by the outside world. An object can be accessed only through its message interface. This saves you from worrying about some foreign code altering your object's instance variables.

Polymorphism is the ability of different objects to react differently to the same message. You need to know about this property so you can take advantage of it when you are designing or writing code.

Inheritance is a programming tool that lets you implement general solutions to a problem in a class and then specialize that solution by creating subclasses. There are many examples of this capability in the Squeak system. Inheritance applies to both variables and methods, but only methods can be overridden.

Jim: Wow, these are some really powerful concepts!

Objective Wizard: Yes, I suggest you learn them as powerful, new concepts and not simply try to fit them into your existing conceptual framework. If you want to use a truly object-oriented programming

JIM	OBJECTIVE WIZARD
	language, you must work with these ideas. They are very much the essence of the paradigm. *Do not* try to learn them by thinking of polymorphism as being "like operator overloading" or methods as being "like procedures." Open up a new space in your imagination, and learn these concepts as something completely new. Do not throw away your old paradigm...just learn to live with two paradigms. You will benefit from both.
I'm still not sure what it means to program in Smalltalk.	
	That is because I have not yet asked you to do any actual programming in Smalltalk. You have written Smalltalk code and you have created some classes, but you have not yet gone through the full programming process. But you will do so soon in forthcoming discussions with me. Good Luck! Auf Wiedersehen.

Summary

New Terms

Encapsulation	Polymorphism
Inheritance	Overriding Inheritance

What Did You Learn?

- What encapsulation is and what it means to you as a programmer.
- What polymorphism is and how to find occurrences of it in the class hierarchy.
- What inheritance is and how to identify it in the class hierarchy.
- What is inherited.
- How to override methods.

Words of Wisdom

Create your subclasses so they make sense. If you can't say with confidence that your subclass is a kind of its superclass, don't use it.

Good inheritance trees are bushy. It's easy to go too far when making subclasses.

Good inheritance schemes rarely go more than four or five classes down from class `Object`.

To Do List

You are a researcher at the Captain Video Memorial Robotics Lab, and your task is to model the behavior of three robot designs. Each design employs a significantly different locomotive strategy.

Robot 1 is a human-like critter that walks on two legs. It changes direction by activating a shape memory alloy muscle. It changes velocity by changing the step rate of its gait.

Robot 2 is a monopod that hops about on one leg and changes direction by pointing its one leg to a different spot when it prepares for landing. It changes velocity by changing its landing angle.

Robot 3 is an amorphous creature that uses a pseudopodic mechanism for locomotion. It changes direction by pumping a fluid into a segment of its pseudopod. It changes velocity by changing the fluid volume in the lead portion of the pseudopod.

Implement each robot design in terms of class definitions and message interfaces. You do not have to implement the method code, but you do have to write a comment describing what each method will do after it is implemented.

When designing your class hierarchy, think in terms of how you can use inheritance to increase code reusability.

When designing your message interfaces, think in terms of behavior. Use polymorphism to facilitate extensibility.

6

Debugging and Testing

Contents at: 'Chapter 6'

#(

debugging
  errors
    Squeak system errors
    compiler errors
    errors from Smalltalk class code
  debugging tools
    notifier
    debugger
  debugging techniques
    embedded code
    separate testing
    stub objects
    message recorders

testing
  timing
  performance changes).

Questions of Interest

- What are Smalltalk code errors like?
- Do conventional debugging strategies work?
- Where does the debugger come from?
- How is the debugger used?
- Is there a particular object-oriented programming style?

Introduction

This chapter is about debugging and testing Smalltalk code. In some aspects, it will be very similar to debugging and testing procedural code in other programming languages; in other ways, it will be new and different. In any case, this chapter does not represent the last word on object-oriented debugging and testing; it is only the beginning.

All debugging processes have their beginnings in an event called an "error." In this chapter, we will discuss the nature of an object-oriented error, where it is detected, and how it is reported to the programmer. As you will soon see, errors can be reported from the compiler during compilation, from the virtual machine, and from Smalltalk code during runtime.

Goals for This Chapter

- To learn about Smalltalk errors, how to find them, and what to do with them after you find them.
- To learn to evaluate the performance of Smalltalk code.

Jim	Objective Wizard
Hey, I need help!	
	Why? What is going on?
Well, I've started to write code, and I have errors.	
	What do you want me to do about them?
Either fix them or teach me how to deal with them.	
	My role in life seems to be teaching you what you need to know about programming in Smalltalk using the Squeak system. Debugging is an important part of Smalltalk programming, so let us talk about it in some detail. How would you like to start?
Error reports are popping up on my screen, and I don't know what they mean. I'm having problems understanding what constitutes a Smalltalk error and how the error is reported to me. I'm getting frustrated. Where's my C++ compiler?	
	Jim, buddy, relax! Insert the following method in your message interface and send it to yourself:

```
relax
"Set physiological parameters to
    relax level"
self bloodPressure: 120/80.
self heartRate: 70.
```

You will be feeling better soon. I never know when to tell humans about Smalltalk debugging. If I tell them too early, they cannot understand its usefulness. If I tell them too late, they have an error attack, like you just had. Humans seem to have no window of opportunity in such matters.

JIM | OBJECTIVE WIZARD

OBJECTIVE WIZARD: Sit back, relax, and listen.

Smalltalk errors can be conveniently categorized by understanding when the error is detected and whence the error report is generated.

There are three sources for error reporting in Smalltalk, as follows:

1. virtual machine
2. `Compiler`
3. Smalltalk code

Let us look at them one at a time.

The virtual machine reports a `doesNotUnderstand:` whenever a receiver object is sent a message that is not in its local or inherited message interface. The virtual machine also reports a `controlBreak`. Both messages are reported to the programmer via the notifier window, Smalltalk's runtime error-reporting mechanism. These messages are generated during runtime.

The compiler reports errors during the compilation process. Compilation occurs whenever you execute code with a **print it (p)** or **do it (d)** menu option or when you save a method in the System Browser or with another tool. The errors are reported by inserting a small error message in reverse video into your code at the point the error was detected.

Smalltalk code can also report an error condition. Although the programmer has little control over the messages reported by the compiler or virtual machine, messages reported from Smalltalk code can be modified, added, or removed.

JIM: Let's begin with the compiler errors. I get those all the time.

OBJECTIVE WIZARD: All right, Jim. Examples of typical compiler errors include the following:

```
Period or right bracket expected
Argument expected
```

JIM | OBJECTIVE WIZARD

```
Unmatched comment quote
Right parenthesis expected
```

The compiler in Squeak will also interactively prompt you for some errors, such as undefined variables.

Compiler errors generally are related to syntax problems. I suggest you follow the steps below to debug a compiler error:

1. Read the error message.
2. Look where it was inserted. The error lies either immediately before or after the inserted error message.
3. Try to identify the error. When you know what it is, press the delete or backspace key to get rid of the error message. Then, fix the code.

If you cannot find the problem, try the following techniques:

1. Comment out a small chunk of code, and then compile it again in an attempt to isolate the error.
2. Check your code for missing end-of-statement periods, missing receiver objects, and typing errors in variable names.

When all else fails, ask someone else to look at your code. The simplest errors are often the most difficult to find!

What about the errors that happen at runtime and pop up a notifier window?

The `error:` method inherited from `Object` is used to report error conditions from Smalltalk code. A list of the methods that send the `error:` message can be generated by selecting `error:` in a System Browser and using the "senders" option on the methods menu.

All error messages reported from Smalltalk code using the `error:` method will display a notifier window.

JIM

OBJECTIVE WIZARD

Very interesting, but what do I do with a notifier when I get one?

A *notifier* is a Squeak window handled by an instance of `Debugger`. It represents two very important pieces of information:

1. Seeing a notifier window means your code has encountered an error condition during runtime.
2. The notifier window's title area has an error message. Read it carefully; it may provide you with the solution to the problem. In many cases, particularly with the `doesNotUnderstand:` error, the notifier will provide all the information you need.

The notifier window also contains a view into the Squeak execution stack. If you cause a user interrupt error (hit the **alt** and period keys on your keyboard), a notifier window will be displayed. The main part of the window will include lines of text that describe pieces of the stack and will look something like the following example:

```
EventSensor>>nextEventFromQueue
EventSensor>>nextEvent
HandMorph>>processEvents
[] in WorldState>>doOneCycleNowFor:
```

Each line of this stack information can be read as some message send to some object. For example, the first line reads: the `nextEventFromQueue` message was sent to the class `EventSensor`.

So how does the information in the notifier window help me fix the error?

Just look at the execution stack information. Start at the top line and work your way down. The first method that is listed and that you wrote is usually where the error occurred. This

JIM	OBJECTIVE WIZARD
	line tends to be the second or third line down the list, but it could be a bit farther down.
I see. What else can I do with the notifier window?	
	When a notifier window is displayed, you have three options, as follows: 1. Solve the problem with information provided by the notifier, close the notifier, and fix the problem. 2. Resume execution from the notifier by selecting the **Proceed** button. You can proceed only from user interrupts and halt errors. 3. Select the **Debug** option in the notifier window, and use the debugger to help you solve the problem.
Yeah! Thanks, I feel as if I can do something now when I get an error condition. What can you tell me about using the debugger?	
	The *Debugger* is a multipane, window-based application that provides you with a group of tools for exploring the code around the reported error. The debugger window has four function areas in four horizontal stripes. The top area replicates the stack information as a list. Selecting an item in the list allows the two bottom areas to show information about that particular bit of the stack. The second area is a row of buttons that allow quick access to common functions. The third area is the best of all; it is the source code that was executing for the part of the stack that was selected when the error occurred. This area is a fully functioning editing area where you can modify and compile code.
That's cool! What about the fourth area?	

JIM | OBJECTIVE WIZARD

Oh, yes, I almost forgot. The fourth area allows you to examine and change the values of variables that are active in the selected part of the stack.

When you are familiar with `Debugger`, try surprising some object with a user interrupt and use the debugger to see what the object was doing.

All right, I'll spend some time looking at the debugger when I get back to the office.

What else can you tell me about debugging in Smalltalk?

I can tell you about a few common debugging techniques, such as these:

1. embedded code
2. separate testing
3. stub objects
4. message recorders

Sounds interesting, but I would appreciate it if you would include some code examples.

Sure.

Using *embedded code* is a technique that makes code participate in its own debugging, which is very much like using embedded debugging code in a procedure or function in any other language.

The kinds of things you can do with embedded code in Smalltalk are as follows:

1. Halt the execution at a particular point in the code.
   ```
   self halt.
   ```
2. Make a noise every time a particular method or statement is executed. Smalltalk is particularly good at making noises. Here is a simple example:
   ```
   SoundPlayer boinkScale.
   ```

JIM	OBJECTIVE WIZARD
	3. Write a string to the Transcript window. `Transcript show: 'some string'.` 4. Keep track of a particular variable or piece of data. Use a Global variable to store the value, and then look at it after the fact.
What do you mean by separate testing?	
	Separate testing means testing each class as you build it. By doing this testing, you ensure that each individual class and its instances work correctly before you combine the classes and instances into an application. I do this testing by opening a Workspace when I start a new class. I put the debugging code and notes into that Workspace until I am finished with the class. This procedure pro vides a sort of running commentary on my development-testing process.
That seems pretty intuitive. What is a stub object?	
	A *stub object* is one whose message interface is identical (or at least similar) to that of some complex object that you have not yet finished. So, you test the code that uses that object before you are ready to finish it.
I don't get it. Wouldn't it be equally difficult to create the stub object as it would be to create the object you haven't finished?	
	Not necessarily. The stub object's methods might return default values or even prompt you for the correct answer.
Hmmm. I wonder if it would be possible to implement a generic stub class?	

JIM | OBJECTIVE WIZARD

Objective Wizard: Yes, it is possible, Jim, but not easy. I suggest that you wait until you have mastered more of Smalltalk and the intricacies of the Squeak class hierarchy before you try to do that.

Jim: Oh, well, in that case, why don't you tell me about message recorders?

Objective Wizard: *Message recorders* simply record any messages they receive. By studying the list of messages, you can tell a great deal about how an object is used. This information is particularly useful in a multiperson development environment.

Unfortunately, creating a generic message recorder requires knowledge and techniques you do not have yet. You can create a partial message recorder by having the messages in which you are interested write information to the Transcript window.

Jim: So, I really can't do either generic stub objects or message recorders now?

Objective Wizard: Correct. They each require the ability to build a generic encapsulator, or something very much like it. That task requires that you work with `ProtoObject` or modify a method in `MetaClass`, so—

Jim: Yow! Hold on! I believe you.

Thanks for the debugging information and strategies.

Before I leave, could you give me some ideas about performance testing and code optimization?

Objective Wizard: Yes, I have some ideas about optimizing Smalltalk code.

My first suggestion is that you implement a performance tester to collect data on the execution of particular code segments. Try the following chunk of code:

```
Time millisecondsToRun: [
1000 timesRepeat: [
   code to test ]]
```

JIM	OBJECTIVE WIZARD
	This sample is a useful piece of code that will answer the number of milliseconds required to execute the code to test 1000 times. The timing precision is limited to the resolution of the system clock.
And how do I change my code to improve performance?	
	Smalltalk executes faster than you might suppose. In my strategy, I wait until near the end of development. Only after I have data to indicate that there is a problem do I concern myself about performance details. Specific changes will be related to specific code, but, in general, I have the following suggestions: 1. Always gather statistics to help locate a performance problem. 2. Focus on optimizing code that gets executed a lot. 3. Caching (keeping available rather than throwing out) graphics images and disk file information can reduce the processing overhead. 4. Sometimes, it will help to change which collection you are using to keep track of groups of objects. Certain collections are faster at certain tasks. For example, an instance of `Set` executes `includes:` messages very quickly, even over large numbers of objects. 5. The kind of number you are using can make a big difference. Often, using floating point numbers is faster than, although not as accurate as, using very large intergers.
Thanks, Wiz. Adios.	
	Vamos a la playa.
No, gracias.	
	Adios.

Summary

New Terms

Notifier	Encapsulator
Debugger	Message Recorder

What Did You Learn?

- Errors are reported by the `Compiler`, by the virtual machine, and from Smalltalk code.
- The `error:` message is used to report errors from Smalltalk code.
- There are heuristics for resolving compiler errors.
- Debugging techniques for Smalltalk are similar to those for other, conventional languages.

Words of Wisdom

Test as you go. Testing a class as you build it saves time and trouble later.

First make it work; then make it fast. Optimizing code as you write wastes time by optimizing code that doesn't need it.

It's never correct the first time. We should not only accept that truism and get accustomed to it, but use it. Iterative refinement gives you a way to turn this truism to your advantage.

Read the information in a notifier window. It's important!

Use a timer to evaluate code performance.

There are several basic heuristics for increasing code performance.

To Do List

Insert the following code in the beginning of a method that you're interested in observing:

```
self halt.
```

One interesting method is `indentationIfBlank:` in `String`.

Send the message that will activate the method you have changed. This should open up a notifier window. Use the notifier menu to open the debugger.

Spend some time poking around in the code and playing with the debugger. Get familiar with this tool, because you will be spending a lot of time with it. Make a list of all the menu options the debugger has, and find out what they do. Write a line or two about each one, and put the notes up on your wall.

As you continue through the next couple of chapters, you should find ample opportunity to use the notifier window and debugger. Be careful: it's easy to get addicted to a good interactive debugging system.

7

The Class Hierarchy

Contents at: 'Chapter 7'

Questions of Interest

- What is a category?
- How are categories named?
- What class and method search techniques are available?
- How does this relate to inheritance?
- What is `ProtoObject`?

Introduction

Squeak is a large system. It includes a rich set of classes that support a wide range of capabilities. Sometimes the size can make it difficult to find a class or method you need. There are sets of tools and techniques to help, although experience and practice will make them less important as you learn the system.

The classes are organized in several ways. As described previously, all classes are part of a superclass-subclass inheritance structure called the class hierarchy. In addition, every class is associated with a category, which groups together related classes regardless of their positions in the class hierarchy. Both of these structures are important in learning to use the system effectively.

Goals for This Chapter

- To understand categories.
- To learn how to find methods and classes of interest.
- To understand the class hierarchy structure.
- To learn a little more about the Squeak development tools.

JIM	OBJECTIVE WIZARD
Aarrggg!	
	Jim! What is wrong?
It's this stupid Squeak system. It's too big! I can't find anything.	
	Jim, relax. It is not as bad as you think.
If it isn't so bad, then why can't I find anything?	
	Because you do not know how to look. What are you trying to find?
Uh...I was trying to build a card game.	
	I see.
You know...just practice to get to know the system. Anyway, I was trying to find a random number generator so I could write some code to shuffle cards.	
	Hmmm...so, how did you search for it?
I didn't really know where to start, so I kind of poked around a lot. I didn't find it, though. There is a random number generator, right?	
	Of course. It is implemented in the class `Random`.
Great, I'll just go and—	
	Wait. You must learn how to find the classes and messages for which you are looking. The Squeak class hierarchy is very rich, and without an idea of how to find what you want you will only frustrate yourself again.
I see what you mean. So what do I do?	

JIM | OBJECTIVE WIZARD

Objective Wizard: Let us start with the class Random. How do you determine which messages it understands?

Jim: I'm not sure. I don't even know how to find it in the browser, even though I know the name of the class.

Objective Wizard: Jim, do you remember your discussion with the Objective Librarian about how classes are organized in Squeak's System Browser?

Jim: Not exactly.

Objective Wizard: The browser is organized by category. Classes know their categories. You can ask them using this category message:

```
Random category
```

This returns a string representing the name of the category. In this case, it is `'Kernel-Numbers'`.

Jim: Okay, what does that mean?

Objective Wizard: That means that the class `Random` is in the category `Kernel-Numbers`. Using naming conventions, class categories are given two layers of information. In this case, the top level is `Kernel`, part of the basic system classes, and the lower level is `Numbers`, which are classes that involve numbers.

Jim: I still don't know how to get a random number.

Objective Wizard: You are an impatient fellow today. Fine, here is a way to get a random number:

```
| rand |
rand := Random new.
rand next.
```

Or, if you would like to use a more object-oriented style, try this:

```
Random new next
```

JIM	OBJECTIVE WIZARD
	Each of these code segments will answer a random number between 0 and 1.
Okay, I guess that's enough.	
	You are more likely to want a random integer.
Right—that would be easier to work with.	
	You can use the `nextInt:` message, which will return a random integer between 1 and the argument. An even easier way is to use the `atRandom` message.
How does that work?	
	You can send the message to an integer to get a random number between 1 and that integer. So, for example, `52 atRandom.` will return a random integer between 1 and 52.
That's great!	
	There are other objects that know how to handle this message.
Okay, what are they?	
	I will not tell you. Instead, I will show you how to find them. But first let us talk about categories again.
Do we have to?	
	Yes. It is important—try to stay focused, Jim. Categories are labels associated with classes. A naming convention allows them to convey two levels of structure. The higher level is the first part of the name, and that is a very good level to know about.
You already said that. But how do I find out what the names mean?	
	There are two ways. You can spend time examining the classes contained in each of the categories and deduce their purpose.

JIM	OBJECTIVE WIZARD
That's less than perfect. What's the other way?	
	Ask.
Ah...umm, so what do they mean?	
	That is a very good question. First, I want to point out that these classes may change as the Squeak system evolves. In particular, there may be more high-level category elements added.
Yeah, I know...no guarantees, implied or otherwise.	
	You have been spending too much time with instances of class `attorney`. Regardless, the names of the top-level categories are as follows:

`Kernel`	Basic system support
`Collections`	Collections (of course)
`Graphics Basic`	Graphics support
`Sound`	Sound support
`Tools`	Development tools
`System`	Compiler and platform
`Network`	Internet things
`VMConstruction`	Virtual machine
`ST80`	Older user interface classes
`Morphic`	Newer user interface classes
`Balloon`	A 2D graphics system
`Balloon3D`	A 3D graphics system
`Speech`	Speech output

The second-level names vary depending on the higher level. Thus, there is a category `Kernel-Numbers`, because numbers are an important aspect of the basic system, but no `Tools-Numbers`, because numbers are too simple to have their own set of development tools.

JIM | OBJECTIVE WIZARD

I could have guessed a lot of those myself. But what is that VM thing?

You might think of it as porting tools. I think of it as a reality translator.

Huh?

Never mind.

I still don't see how all this is going to tell me which objects can use the atRandom method.

Very well. Give me a moment. I will be using some ideas you have not yet seen. Just watch, and do not worry if you do not understand everything.

Right, I'm ready.

We will find all the methods in the system that have names that contain the substring 'random'. First, here is the code that will check to see if a message might involve random numbers:

```
(#atRandom asLowerCase)
   includesSubString: 'random'.
```

This code will return true if the method name includes 'random' and false otherwise. The next step is to list all the classes in the system. This code will return all of the classes we care about right now:

```
Object withAllSubclasses.
```

Once we have a class, the names of the methods in that class can be accessed with the selectors message. For example,

```
Integer selectors.
```

will return the names of the methods in Integer. Finally, put everything together, as follows, using some things you have not seen yet:

JIM | OBJECTIVE WIZARD

```
Object withAllSubclasses do:
    [:clas | clas selectors do:
    [:sel |
     (sel asLowercase
      includesSubString:'random')
        ifTrue: [
            Transcript
                show: clas name;
                show: ' ';
                show: selector;
                cr]]].
```

This code will list all the methods in the system that contain `'random'` in their names. Oh, make sure you have a Transcript window open.

So what does that tell us?

In this case, it will list a number of interesting methods. Among them are the methods `atRandom` for both `Integer` and `SequenceableCollection`.

Okay, that's good to know.

Of course, it is much easier simply to use the Method Finder tool, to which the Objective Librarian introduced you in your second visit with her.

What! You mean we went through all that for nothing? Why didn't you remind me that there was a tool for this to start with?

What would be the fun in that? Besides, the Objective Librarian emphasized the importance of your visit to the library as a reference to which you could look back, particularly when it comes to Squeak's tools.

Grrr. While I look back fondly at my time with her, I can't remember every little thing. I—you know—might have been a bit distracted.

JIM | OBJECTIVE WIZARD

Okay, so what about finding a class that includes the word `'random'`.

That is easier, although it still includes things you have not yet seen, such as this:

```
Object withAllSubclasses do:
    [:clas |
     (clas name asLowercase
      includesSubString:'random')
      ifTrue: [
          Transcript
              show: clas name;
              cr]].
```

That's not too hard...

Or you could do the same thing using the **find class** menu option.

I saw that one coming. So, where is this find class thing?

It is in the System Browser. You should spend time with the System Browser. Learn what is on the menus and what each tool does. There are many tools there to help you find things you need. Pay particular attention to the cross-reference tools.

I can do that. Thanks, I think. What should I do now?

Look around and learn. Soon you will know where many useful things are and how to find everything you need.

Sounds good. See you later.

Hey Wiz! You around?

Jim? I did not expect you back so soon.

Yeah, well I'm kind of confused about something.

Tell me, and I will try to clarify it for you.

JIM | OBJECTIVE WIZARD

Jim: I'm still playing around with the idea of a card game, and I'm ready to shuffle the deck.

Objective Wizard: And?

Jim: Well, I found a method called `shuffled`. I'd like to use it, but it's in `SequenceableCollection`.

Objective Wizard: So, what is the problem?

Jim: I'm not sure if I should copy and paste the code or try to use `SequenceableCollection` instead.

Objective Wizard: You are a bit confused. Let us review some concepts. This time, we will discuss them in terms of the classes with which you are working.

Remember we had an idea called *inheritance*.

Jim: Of course, that's where one class gets methods and variables from another class.

Objective Wizard: Yes. A class inherits the methods and the definition of variables from its superclass. You can ask a class about its superclass. That is done using the `superclass` message. Try it.

Jim: Me? Okay...

```
Array superclass.
```

That tells me its superclass is `ArrayedCollection`.

Objective Wizard: Very good. Now, what is the superclass of its superclass?

Jim: Let's see.

```
(Array superclass)
    superclass.
```

JIM	OBJECTIVE WIZARD
Which is... `SequenceableCollection`!	
	Very good. So what does that mean for the `shuffled` message?
It's in `SequenceableCollection`, so it is inherited by `ArrayedCollection`. And then `Array` inherits it from `ArrayedCollection`?	
	Yes. Inheritance does not stop one level down.
But how would I have found which objects inherited the method from `SequenceableCollection`?	
	One way to accomplish that task is to learn more about the subclasses of `SequenceableCollection` by sending it messages. You could have seen all of its subclasses by sending this message: `SequenceableCollection allSubclasses.` This message returns a rather large list of classes that are direct or indirect subclasses.
So, all of those classes inherit the `shuffled` method?	
	Yes, although some may choose to override it.
You said one way—are there others?	
	One other way is to use the browse hierarchy option in the System Browser.
Another menu option I should check out?	
	Yes.

JIM | OBJECTIVE WIZARD

Jim: So, that piece of code you wrote earlier—the one that gets all the classes—how did that work?

Objective Wizard: You mean this:

```
Object withAllSubclasses.
```

Jim: That's the one.

Objective Wizard: It returns a list of most of the classes in the Squeak system. `Object` is the superclass for all the normal classes, so asking for a list including it and all of its subclasses will return all of the classes you normally care about. There is a sort of raw, primordial class called `ProtoObject`, which is the superclass of `Object`, and a few other classes that do not want to inherit from `Object` for one reason or another.

Jim: So the other subclasses of `ProtoObject` are uncivilized?

Objective Wizard: You mean that as a joke, but it is not far from the truth. I would say that they are untamed or unconstrained, rather than uncivilized. This is not something with which you, as a newcomer to ObjectLand, should be concerned.

Jim: Anything else?

Objective Wizard: In the ObjectLand library, there is an alphabetical list of classes that lists each class, superclass and category. You may find it useful, although it may change as Squeak—

Jim: Yeah, I know. No guarantees expressed or implied.

Objective Wizard: Exactly, and please stop spending so much time browsing the class `attorney`.

Jim: That's probably good advice.

Objective Wizard: It is. I am sure I will see you later. Au revoir.

Summary

New Terms

Category ProtoObject

What Did You Learn?

- How to find methods and classes whose names contain particular substrings.
- What categories are and how their names are structured.
- The places of `Object` and `ProtoObject` in the class hierarchy.
- A little more about some of the development tools.
- How random numbers are accessed and used.

Words of Wisdom

Spend time learning about the tools for finding things. New versions of Squeak may contain new classes and restructure old ones, but the tools and techniques will remain essentially the same.

You do not need to know about every class or even every category to do something useful.

If you are using a class, you should know its superclass and subclasses.

At first, you'll spend most of your time searching for things. As you become more experienced, your time will shift toward more doing and less searching. However, you will never completely stop searching.

To Do List

Find the category and superclass of each of the following classes:

```
Cursor
TextColor
Semaphore
AbstractScoreEvent
BorderedMorph
Model
```

Find all the subclasses of `Number` and of `BitBlt`.

List the classes that implement methods that include the substring `'drago'` in their names.

Look through the categories in the System Browser. Can you guess the kinds of classes each category contains? Look through the classes in a few categories to check your guesses.

8

Numbers et al.

Contents at: 'Chapter 8'

#(

the `Magnitude` hierarchy

```
Magnitude
  Character
  Date
  LookupKey
    Association
  Number
    Float
    Fraction
    Integer
  Time
```

kind of numbers
- integers
- floating point
- fractions

number crunching issues
- order of execution
- mixed mode math
- fractions based on integers
- floating point operations

polymorphism revisited).

Questions of Interest

- What are the math capabilities of Squeak?
- What is the order of execution?
- What about mixed mode arithmetic?

Introduction

Numerical manipulation is a very common programming task. Many computer programming languages were created solely to provide a way to perform large amounts of "number crunching." While Smalltalk is not one of those languages, it does have very sophisticated numeric manipulation capabilities.

Because everything in Smalltalk is an object, it follows directly that numbers are represented as objects and that arithmetic is done by sending messages. This greatly influences how numbers are handled in Smalltalk.

One of the important differences between handling numbers in Squeak and in other systems is that the behavior of numbers is defined within a higher level of abstraction found in the class `Magnitude`. By learning about numbers, you will learn quite a bit about how to deal with some of the other subclasses of `Magnitude`, such as `Date`, `Time`, and `Character`.

The `Number` class itself is an abstraction; the actual numbers are represented by instances of subclasses of `Number`, such as `Float`, `Fraction`, and `Integer`.

Goals for This Chapter

- To implement mathematical expressions in Smalltalk.
- To see how the underlying characteristics and order of execution shape the behavior of the numerical capabilities of Squeak.
- To get a feel for the capabilities and limitations of Squeak's current numeric manipulation system and an understanding of its extensibility.

Jim	Objective Wizard
Hi, I'm back again!	
	I am busy right now. Is there any chance you could come back later?
Well, I've come a long way.	
	All right, all right, what do you want to know about?
How about numbers? I need to do some arithmetic, and I'm not sure how to do it in Smalltalk.	
	How serendipitous! I happen to be working in the `Magnitude` class hierarchy at this very picomoment. I am considering extending some of its capabilities.
Oh...but I want to know about numbers, not magnitudes.	
	I understand, Jim, but you do not. Remember that, in Smalltalk, all objects are defined in classes and that all classes reside somewhere in the class hierarchy. Remember also that classes inherit variables and methods from their superclasses and pass variables and methods on to their subclasses.

Take a look at the `Magnitude` hierarchy. There are actually more subclasses of class `Magnitude`, but, for the purposes of the moment, notice that `Float`, `Fraction`, and `Integer` are subclasses of `Number`, which in turn is a subclass of `Magnitude`. Also notice, in the code below, that there are other subclasses of `Magnitude`:

```
Magnitude
    Character
    Date
    LookupKey
       Association
    Number
       Float
       Fraction
       Integer
    Time
```

JIM	OBJECTIVE WIZARD
	Notice that all the specific number classes (`Float`, `Integer`, and `Fraction`) are subclasses of class `Number`.
	The reasons for this arrangement can best be understood by discussing the inheritance architecture of this hierarchy. Let us start with the superclass of this hierarchy, class `Magnitude`.
	Class `Magnitude` is an abstract class implemented to handle the comparing, ordering, and interval testing of instances of its subclasses. If you are interested in answers to questions such as Is 324 less than –123? Is 43 between 17 and 33? Is Aug 4, 2001 later than Jun 2, 2001? Is 2:17 later than 1:24? Does M come after K? then class `Magnitude` provides the protocol for instances of its subclasses to make these kinds of comparisons. Since class `Magnitude` is an abstract class, it is intended to be a container of capability and protocol and is not intended to be instantiated. In this case, the subclasses of `Magnitude` must implement many of the capabilities described in `Magnitude`.
So `Magnitude` has the protocol for comparing instances of its subclasses. What about the subclasses? Pretty good question, eh?	

	Adequate question. The immediate subclasses are as follows:
	
	`Character`
	`Date`
	`LookupKey`
	`Number`
	`Time`

JIM	OBJECTIVE WIZARD
	While I enjoy talking about all the classes in ObjectLand, I will, for the sake of brevity, outline the capabilities of each of these classes and then will focus on only `Number` and its subclasses.
	Class `LookupKey` is primarily of interest as the parent class of `Association`. Class `Association` associates two objects in a particular direction. It is rarely used directly but is heavily used by the `Dictionary` classes. You do not need to be concerned with `Association`. You will benefit from its existence but will probably never use it directly.
	Characters in Squeak are represented as instances of the class `Character`. Its instances represent characters from the extended ASCII set from ASCII value 0 to 255.
	Class `Date` is used to represent dates and includes methods for querying and manipulating the date. I suggest that you look at the method list for `Date`. Start by looking at the `today` class method.
	Class `Time` is used to represent the time of day and includes methods for querying and manipulating times. I suggest you look at the method list for `Time`. Start by looking at the `now` class method.
	Class `Number` is an abstract class that establishes the general behavior of "numberness." Class `Number` is never used directly. It provides, through inheritance, the general structure for all numbers in the system.
That's all very interesting, but I have particular tasks that I need to do with numbers, and I want to make sure that Squeak can handle my needs. If I asked you some specific questions, would you answer them?	
	Silly human! Have I not answered all your questions up to this point?
Yes, Wizard, but I want very specific answers this time	

Jim	Objective Wizard

Jim: because arithmetic is important in my application.

Objective Wizard: Very well, I will answer your questions in the most specific form I know, which is Smalltalk code. In return, I want you to read each expression carefully, in the manner I have already taught you. I will also show you what is returned from each expression.

Will that be adequate?

Jim: Wonderful.

(3 + 4) × 22

Objective Wizard:

Code	Returned Value
`3 + 4 * 22`	`154`

Jim: What? You got the correct answer, but it looks like it should evaluate to 91.

Objective Wizard: No, I got it right. You just read it wrong. You read it as if it were an arithmetic expression and computed along the conventional rules for evaluating arithmetic expressions.

Here, let me read it as a Squeak expression for you:

Send the + message to the integer object `3`, with the integer object `4` as an argument. This message send returns the integer object `7`, to which the message `*` with the integer object `22` is then sent as an argument. This message send returns an integer object `154`.

Notice that both the message sends in this expression are binary. According to the order of evaluation, the `+` message will be sent first and then the `*` message. In Squeak, all arithmetic expressions are evaluated according to the order of evaluation. In some cases, the result will differ from the conventional arithmetic order of evaluation.

Jim: Oh, I see. I will remember that and improve my Squeak code reading habits. Thank you.

JIM	OBJECTIVE WIZARD
How about doing some more arithmetic for me?	
	What would you like me to do?
F = C (1.8) + 32 Where C = 20.	

Code	Returned Value
`C := 20.`	
`F := C * (1.8) + 32.`	68

$A^2 + B^2$

Where A = 7 and B = 9.

Code	Returned Value
`7 squared + 9 squared.`	130

$\tan^{-1}(\cos(X) + \sin(1 - X))$

Where X = 0.6 radians.

Code	Returned Value
`| x |`	
`x := 0.6.`	
`(x cos + (1-x) sin)`	
`arcTan.`	0.882061

How about doing that for X = 45 degrees?

Code	Returned Value
`| x |`	
`x := 45 degreesToRadians.`	
`(x cos + (1-x) sin)`	
`arcTan.`	0.743791

If you want the answer in degrees, use the `radiansToDegrees` message.

JIM	OBJECTIVE WIZARD

n! / r!

For five things (n) taken three (r) at a time.

Code	Returned Value

`| n r |`
`n := 5.`
`r := 3.`
`n factorial /`
`   r factorial.`
	20

Hmmm, not bad. Tell me more about the individual subclasses of class `Number`.

Class `Float` implements the arithmetic operations on floating point numbers. The precision of floating point numbers in Squeak depends on the hardware and operating system with which you are working.

Class `Integer` implements the arithmetic operations on integer numbers. Actually, `Integer` is an abstract class with three subclasses: `LargePositiveInteger`, `LargeNegativeInteger`, and `SmallInteger`. Now that I have mentioned this information, feel free to forget it. The conversion between the different kinds of integers is automatic. Integers in Squeak can get quite large. Try this piece of code, which computes the factorial of 100:

```
| answer |
answer := 1.
1 to: 100 do: [:num |
   answer := answer * num].
^answer.
```

This code will return a large integer. To see how large, replace the last line with the following code:

```
^answer printString size.
```

This code will return the number of digits in the answer.

JIM	OBJECTIVE WIZARD
	Class `Fraction` implements the arithmetic operations on rational numbers (fractions). Since the numerator and denominator are both represented as integers, fractions can be very precise, much more precise than the hardware-based floating point numbers.
Are there any heuristics for learning to use arithmetic in Squeak?	
	Yes, try these four heuristics: 1. Remember that there are unary, binary, and keyword messages in the `Number` classes, and the type of message sent will affect the order of evaluation. When in doubt, use parentheses. 2. Mixed mode arithmetic is allowed. The result will be determined by the arithmetic functions that are used. Usually, the answer moves to the most general kind of number in the expression, with fractions more general than integers, and floats more general than either integers or fractions. 3. The arithmetic capabilities of the system are extensible. In other words, if a capability does not exist, you can create it. 4. Floating point math is based on the capabilities of the underlying processor.
I think I've got it. I'm ready to write some code.	
	Then I will see you later. Do not forget the To Do List positioned just beyond the end of our discussion. Arrivederci.
Arrivederci, indeed!	

Summary

New Terms

Rational Number (Fraction)

What Did You Learn?

- Arithmetic in Smalltalk is similar to but different from arithmetic in other languages.
- The normal Smalltalk order of execution is used for arithmetic.
- Parentheses are useful for making arithmetic expressions more readable.
- The mathematical operations are implemented in Smalltalk methods.
- The mathematical operations are changeable and extensible.
- New number systems can be implemented with new subclasses of `Number`.
- Implementing numeric expressions in Smalltalk is a piece of cake.
- The message interface to the `Number` classes is extensive.

Words of Wisdom

Remember the order of execution! Subtle bugs can creep into your code if you don't keep that in mind. If you're not sure, use parentheses.

There is nothing sacred about the methods in the `Number` classes. If you have a good reason to change one, then change it. If you have a good reason to add one, then add it.

To Do List

Write a method in `Number` that will answer the receiver incremented by 1. Write a similar method that will decrement the receiver by 1.

You work for NASA (National Aeronautics and Space Administration). Your job is multidimensional software support:

1. You must extend the math capabilities of Squeak to meet NASA needs.
2. You must implement selected formulas in Smalltalk.
3. You must create tools for the local applied mathematicians and physicists.

Your first requests for extending the mathematical capabilities of Squeak involve adding some unit conversion methods:

`fahrenheitToKelvin`	Answer degrees Kelvin from Fahrenheit
`lightYearsToMillimeters`	Answer millimeters from light-years
`yearsToSeconds`	Answer seconds from years

The speed of light is about 3.0×10^{10} centimeters per second. The Kelvin temperature scale uses the same degree size as that of the Celsius scale, but the 0 point for Kelvin is absolute zero (–273° C).

A new laser-based system has been installed at NASA to provide communications with space probes and exploration platforms. Write some Smalltalk code that will answer the round trip speed-of-light communications delay. Specify some space objects that have interesting distances from Earth. As a test, you should get a delay of about 2.567 seconds for communicating with Tyco Moonbase (384,068 kilometers away). Question: Should the returned object be an instance of `Time`?

Engineers are asking you for an extension to the `Number` classes to handle complex numbers. Design such a system by creating a class definition and a message interface list. If you have time, start on the implementation. Remember that a complex number has an imaginary part and a real part, just as a fraction has a numerator and denominator.

9

Collections

Contents at: 'Chapter 9'

Questions of Interest

- How can I store and manipulate objects?
- How do I create a container?

- How do I put things into my container?
- Can I change containers?
- Can I make a new kind of container?
- Why would I want to make a new kind of container?

Introduction

One of the first things a novice Smalltalk programmer notices is the rich set of collections Squeak supports. The polymorphic nature of Smalltalk and the lack of typing makes the collections truly generic. They don't need to be reimplemented for every kind of object they contain.

Because collections have a common message interface, the choice of what collection to use can often be put off until more is known about the needs of the user and application code. This capability allows for simple initial implementations with growth to greater complexity when appropriate.

Conversion messages represent another capability of the `Collection` hierarchy. As you will soon discover, conversion messages allow you to easily convert one type of collection to another and then back again.

Goals for This Chapter

- To know what collections are implemented in Smalltalk and where to find them.
- To understand the capabilities and limitations of the more common collections well enough to make an informed choice when one is needed.
- To understand the ways the collections differ from one another, and the ways they are the same.
- To learn to use collections within your own applications.

JIM | OBJECTIVE WIZARD

Hey, Wiz, I have an emergency. Can you help me?

Certainly. I have been waiting for you. I was concerned that you had quit before I had the opportunity to tell you about collections in Smalltalk.

Well, data structures are the reason I'm back. Much of my work revolves around the containment and manipulation of data.

In Smalltalk, the interesting data structures are implemented as subclasses of `Collection`, so instead of talking about data structures, we talk about collections.

Sounds like what I want.

Then hold on to your keyboard, buddy. You are about to get excited. Smalltalk has a really interesting array (pun intended) of collections. Here is a partial view of the `Collection` hierarchy:

```
Collection
   Bag
   SequenceableCollection
      ArrayedCollection
         Array
         ByteArray
         String
      OrderedCollection
         SortedCollection
   Interval
   Set
      Dictionary
         IdentityDictionary
```

All these classes are collections, in the sense that they contain and manipulate objects. Each subclass of `Collection` is either a data structure for your use or a holder of functionality to be inherited. `Collection`, `SequenceableCollection`, and `ArrayedCollection` are abstract classes, which you

JIM | OBJECTIVE WIZARD

will not directly use. All the other classes listed above will be useful to you. Some of them will be used soon and often, we will cover those classes first.

What do you think about discussing what they have in common, and then talking about each one separately with examples?

Sounds great! I'm all ears.

The collection classes have a common message interface. This commonality means that there is a set of messages that every collection can handle, and you do not have to know which collection you are dealing with in order to use them.

The first set of messages I want to mention are the iteration messages. These messages give you a way of executing a piece of code for each element in the collection. The iteration messages are as follows:

```
do:
select:
reject:
collect:
detect:
inject:into:
```

We will discuss these messages when we meet to discuss booleans and blocks.

There are also some messages for testing whether or not a particular object is in a collection:

```
includes:
occurrencesOf:
```

The `includes:` answers `true` if the collection contains at least one occurrence of the object passed as an argument. The `occurrencesOf:` message answers how many occurrences of the object passed as an argument are in the collection.

Some messages that you can send will tell you things about the collection as a whole. These messages are as follows:

JIM | OBJECTIVE WIZARD

```
isEmpty
notEmpty
size
```

The `isEmpty` and `notEmpty` messages will answer `true` or `false` depending on whether the collection has any elements in it.

Jim: That's straightforward enough.

The `size` message will answer the number of elements in the collection.

Jim: These messages will work for any collection?

Yes, even those we do not discuss. The subclasses of `Collection` we will be discussing are

```
Bag
Array
String
OrderedCollection
SortedCollection
Set
Dictionary
```

Jim: That's a lot of collections. How will I decide which one to use?

There are some good comparison criteria that will facilitate decision making.

Jim: Great. What are they?

Try asking yourself the following sequence of questions:

1. Do I need a fixed-size or variable-size collection? In other words, do I want my collection to grow as more data are added, or do I want it always to be the same size as I specified when I created it?
2. Do I need an indexed data structure? In other words, do I want to index into my data structure to reach the object at some location?

JIM | OBJECTIVE WIZARD

3. How do I want to access my data objects? This question is tied in with the indexing criteria since a collection that cannot be indexed allows the user a very limited number of ways to find out what it contains.
4. How do I want to add objects to and remove objects from my data structure? You have many choices here, the most important of which is whether you want to just toss objects into the collection or to put them in specific places.
5. Do I want to store multiple occurrences of an object in my data structure? In other words, will I be adding the same object multiple times?
6. Are there any special capabilities or restrictions I should be taking into account? (You will find out more about these as we describe each collection.)

Let's start with `Bag`! Show me your bag of tricks.

```
self laugh: 3
```

Ha, ha, ha.

Class `Bag` is modeled after a physical bag, such as the kind they give you at a grocery store. You can put things into a bag and take things back out, but there is no real structure. A bag is just a clump of objects with no particular organization.

Here is how a `Bag` stacks up under our list of criteria:

Questions	Answers
Fixed Size?	No
Indexed?	No
Access?	None
Add and Remove?	`add:, remove:`
Multiple Occurrences?	Yes

Below is an example of `Bag` used as a sales monitor in a music store. This bag holds all the sales for a given day.

```
SaleMonitor := Bag new.
```

JIM	OBJECTIVE WIZARD
	Sales personnel add sales to the bag in the following way:

```
SaleMonitor
   add: 'Jimmy Buffett';
   add: 'Bach';
   add: 'Jimmy Buffett';
   add: 'Hank Snow';
   add: 'Cindy Lauper';
   add: 'V.A.S.T.';
   add: 'Moby'.
```

If management asks for sales information, such as how many sales were made today, the query would be done in this manner:

How many sales were made today?

```
SaleMonitor size.
```

If you need to know how many Jimmy Buffett CDs sold today, the following is the code you would write:

```
SaleMonitor
   occurrencesOf:'Jimmy Buffett'.
```

Were there any sales today?

```
SaleMonitor notEmpty.
```

What's next?

Class `Array` is next. It is very similar to the conventional implementation of an array. In Smalltalk, an `Array` is a collection with a fixed number of places for you to insert objects.

Like an egg carton?

Yes, perhaps that is an apt analogy.

Here are vital statistics of `Array`:

Questions	Answers
Fixed Size?	Yes
Indexed?	Yes
Access?	`at:, first, last`
Add and Remove?	`at:put:`
Multiple Occurrences?	Yes

JIM | OBJECTIVE WIZARD

Jim: Sure, I've worked with arrays in other languages. The only difference seems to be that arrays in Smalltalk can hold any kind of object.

Say, does that mean I can put collections inside other collections?

Objective Wizard: Yes, it does. Any object really means *any* object. You can even put a collection inside itself.

Jim: Weird.

Objective Wizard: It seems perfectly natural to me and to the other residents of ObjectLand. Soon, it will be second nature to you, too.

Let us make an instance of `Array` and experiment with it.

```
A :=  Array new: 4.
```

We have just created an array that can contain four objects. To put some objects in the array, we will use the `at:put:` message.

```
A  at: 1 put: 100;
   at: 2 put: 200;
   at: 3 put: 'Hi';
   at: 4 put: 'There'.
```

I have a question for you, Jim. What was in the array before we executed this last piece of code?

Jim: Hmm...I'm not sure. I would guess there was nothing in it.

Objective Wizard: Sorry, Jim. Here is the correct answer:

Any variable, or in this case element, in an array that has not yet been assigned—or set a value with an `at:put:` message—contains the `nil` object. This statement holds true for most of the fixed-size collections.

Jim: Most?

JIM | OBJECTIVE WIZARD

Objective Wizard: Yes, some collections are designed to contain only particular kinds of objects. For example, a ByteArray can contain only the integers from 0 to 255, and instances of String can contain only characters. Try the following to see what these two classes use as default values:

```
(ByteArray new: 4) at: 1.
(String new: 4) at: 1.
```

Jim: I'll try that when I get back to the office.

Objective Wizard: Let us continue.

Now that we have an array, let us send it some messages, as follows:

Code	Value
`A at: 3.`	`'Hi'`
`A isEmpty.`	`false`
`A size.`	`4`
`A includes: 99.`	`false`
`A occurrencesOf:'Hi'.`	`1`
`A at: 2 put: 99.`	`99`
`A last.`	`'There'`
`A at: 2.`	`99`

I should remind you of something that we talked about quite a while ago. An instance of Array can be created by using a shortcut syntax. We could have created and initialized our original array by doing the following:

```
A := #(100 200 'Hi' 'There').
```

Jim: Strings are next. I don't normally think of them as a data structures. You did say they could contain only characters, didn't you?

Objective Wizard: Yes, I did. Instances of String are very much like arrays that contain only characters. Strings have a sort of split personality. From one point of view, a string is a collection, with

JIM | OBJECTIVE WIZARD

all the normal collection behaviors. From another point of view, a string is a single object that has a message interface designed for dealing with strings. Smalltalk handles this by making `String` a subclass of `Collection`, and then enhances it with a special syntax and a lot of extra messages.

Here is how `String` fits into our criteria:

Questions	Answers
Fixed Size?	Yes
Indexed?	Yes
Access?	`at:,first, last`
Add and Remove?	`at:put:`
Multiple Occurrences?	Yes
Restriction?	Characters only

So, strings are like arrays that have some extra string handling messages. Could you show me some of those extra messages?

Certainly. Here are some messages to strings:

Code	Returned Value
`'abcd'asUppercase`	`'ABCD'`
`'AMBER'reversed`	`'REBMA'`
`'-47'asInteger`	`-47`
`'Hi' >='Ho'`	`false`

Now let us do some code that will treat a string as if it were a collection.

```
A := String new: 4.
A at: 1 put: $h;
  at: 2 put: $o;
  at: 3 put: $m;
  at: 4 put: $e.
```

JIM | OBJECTIVE WIZARD

Code	Returned Value
`A at: 3`	`$m`
`A at: 1 put: $d`	`$d`
`A first`	`$d`
`A includes: $K`	`false`
`A occurrencesOf: $o`	`1`
`A size`	`4`

Interesting! I can switch back and forth between treating strings as strings and treating them as if they were collections. That could be handy.

All right, I'm ready for the next one.

Instead of one, I think I will give you two examples and cover both `OrderedCollection`, perhaps the most generally useful collection in ObjectLand, and `SortedCollection`.

OrderedCollection is like an array that will grow to be as large as necessary. You can increase its size by adding new objects to the front or back of the collection.

SortedCollection is the same as an `OrderedCollection`, except that the order is determined by a sorting strategy.

The following is the basic information for `OrderedCollection`:

Questions	Answers
Fixed Size?	No
Indexed?	Yes
Access?	`at:`, `first`, `last`
Add and Remove?	`at:put:`, `add:` `remove:`
Multiple Occurrences?	Yes

JIM	OBJECTIVE WIZARD

The basics for `SortedCollection` are similar, as you can see here:

Questions	Answers
Fixed Size?	No
Indexed?	Yes
Access?	`at:,first,last`
Add and Remove?	`add:,remove:`
Multiple Occurrences?	Yes
Capability?	Sorting
Restriction?	Sorting strategy

Jim: Why is "sorting strategy" given as a restriction?

Objective Wizard: Sorted collections use something called a sort block to decide whether or not two objects are in the correct order. The default sort block simply uses the <= message. If you try to add an object that the sort block cannot handle, you will get a notifier window signaling an error.

Jim: So, I have to be certain that the objects in the collection can handle the <= message; otherwise, I need to create a new sort block.

How do I create a sort block?

Objective Wizard: *Sort blocks* are simply two-argument blocks that answer `true` if the first and second arguments are in the correct order and `false` if they are not. We will discuss blocks later, when we discuss booleans and blocks.

Jim: How about some examples of these two kinds of collections?

Objective Wizard: Fine.

Let's begin by creating one of each collection.

```
A := OrderedCollection new.
S := SortedCollection new.
```

JIM	OBJECTIVE WIZARD

Code	Returned Value
`A add: 10.`	`10`
`A add: 11.`	`11`
`A addFirst: 44.`	`44`
`A asArray.`	`#(44 10 11)`
`A first.`	`44`
`S addAll: A.`	
`S asArray.`	`#(10 11 44)`
`A at: 2 put: 1.`	`1`
`A removeFirst`	`44`
`S addAll: A.`	
`S asArray.`	`#(1 7 11 11 44)`
`S removeFirst.`	`1`

That `asArray` message looks interesting. Are there any others like it?

Yes, there are. I will talk about them after we cover the rest of the collections.

Sets are next, aren't they? Are they anything like the sets I learned about in my math classes?

Yes and yes. Instances of `Set` act very much the same as the sets you learned about in school.

Here is the basic information for `Set`:

Questions	Answers
Fixed Size?	No
Indexed?	No
Access?	None
Add and Remove?	`add:`, `remove:`
Multiple Occurrences?	No

Note that sets will not contain multiple occurrences of an object. I believe I can make that statement more clear with the following example:

JIM | OBJECTIVE WIZARD

Code	Returned Value
`A := Set new`	`Set()`
`A add: 10.`	`10`
`A add: 9.`	`9`
`A add: 10.`	`10`
`A size.`	`2`
`A.`	`Set(9 10)`

Jim: Oh. Sets are just like bags, except they don't keep multiple occurrences. Does that mean that the `occurrencesOf:` message always answers `1` when sent to a set?

Objective Wizard: An excellent question! The `occurrencesOf:` message will always answer `1` if the argument is in the set, and will answer `0` if it is not.

Jim: What's next?

Objective Wizard: `Dictionary` is a very interesting collection.

Unlike all the other collections we have talked about, *Dictionary* stores sets of relationships between two objects. The relationship associates a key object with a value object. Once the relationship has been entered, you can access the value object if you know the associated key object.

Here is our criteria information:

Questions	Answers
Fixed Size?	No
Indexed?	Yes (any object)
Access?	`at:`
Add and Remove?	`at:put:`, `removeKey:`
Multiple Occurrences?	No for keys Yes for values

Jim: I'm not sure I understand.

JIM	OBJECTIVE WIZARD
	It is easier to show you than to explain. `D := Dictionary new.`

Code	Returned Value
D at: 'one' put: 1.	1
D at: 'two' put: 2.	2
D at: 'zero' put: 0.	0
D at: 1 put: 'one'.	'one'
D at: 2 put: 'two'.	'two'
D size.	5
D at: 2.	'two'
D at: 'two'.	2
D occurrencesOf: 2.	1
D removeKey: 'one'.	
D size.	4

With an instance of class `Dictionary`, when you are talking about one of the objects it contains, you are talking about a value, not a key. This statement means that messages such as `includes:` and `do:` apply only to the values in the dictionary.

Now, you were going to say more about that `asArray` and similar messages.

Yes, I will do that now.

You can easily switch between collections by means of one of the conversion messages. A *conversion message* creates a copy of the collection to which it is sent but translates it into a different kind of collection during the copying process.

This translation would be not be very useful if it were not for the fact that the copied collection takes on the attributes of the new collection. For example, look at the following chart:

Code	Returned Value
'Hello' size.	5
'Hello' asSet size.	4
'Hi' asArray.	($H $i)
#(1 2 3 2 1) asSet.	Set(3 2 1)

JIM | OBJECTIVE WIZARD

Wizard: The process of converting a collection to a set squishes out all the duplicates. Similar things happen during conversions to other kinds of collections. Below is a list of some of the collection conversion messages included in Smalltalk. You can, of course, add more if you wish.

```
asArray
asBag
asOrderedCollection
asSet
asSortedCollection
```

Jim: Neat! Now I know how to contain and organize my information, but why isn't there a way to store data in a disk file?

Wizard: But there is, Jim.

Jim: Well, what is it, Wizard?

Wizard: There are several classes involved in the storing of data in files. But we must discuss `Stream` and its subclasses first.

A *stream* can be thought of as a collection having another point of view. It does several collectionlike things, such as containing groups of objects and preserving an order within that group; yet, a stream's intent is different from the intent of a collection. Streams have a more dynamic view of data than do collections.

Each stream works with a collection. We use the term "streaming over a collection" to describe this relationship. The stream keeps track of a position within the collection, and that position controls which part of the collection it will affect when you send the stream messages.

I believe an example is in order:

```
S := ReadWriteStream on: #(1 2).
```

Jim	Objective Wizard

Code	Returned Value
`S next.`	`1`
`S next.`	`2`
`S atEnd.`	`true`
`S reset.`	
`S next.`	`1`
`S position.`	`1`
`S nextPut: 7.`	`7`
`S nextPut: 8.`	`8`
`S contents.`	`(1 7 8)`
`S nextPutAll: 'AB'.`	`'AB'`
`S contents.`	`(1 7 8 $A $B)`

As you can see, streams work with one position of their underlying collections at a time. They also have messages that examine their current positions and can change the current positions. There are many more messages that we can not take the time to examine now. I suggest you use a System Browser to look at more of the `Stream` message interface.

I'll look when we're finished, but what does this have to do with disk files?

I think I can answer that by showing you some of the `Stream` class hierarchy:

```
Stream
   PositionableStream
      ReadStream
      WriteStream
         ReadWriteStream
            FileStream
```

I am sure that the last class, `FileStream`, will be of particular interest to you. Instead of working with an underlying collection, file streams use an underlying disk file.

File streams are a little different from the other streams. The primary difference is that they can handle only characters. They also have several messages that do not apply to the other `Stream` subclasses; for example, the message `close`.

JIM | OBJECTIVE WIZARD

One way to create a file stream is to use the class message `fileNamed:`, as follows:

```
S := FileStream fileNamed:
   'MyFile.txt'.
```

The argument to this message can be a fully qualified path name.

You now have a file stream over an open file with the position set at the beginning of the file (which is zero). You can send any of the stream messages to read, write, or modify the file contents. When you are done working with the file, do the following:

```
S close.
```

This code will close the file and take care of any necessary odds and ends.

We will talk more about files and streams, including some very useful streams for reading objects from and writing objects to files, in just a few chapters.

Jim: Good.

I think I can figure out the disk file stuff now. I'd better go. My brain is full.

Objective Wizard: All right. Shalom.

Jim: Shalom for now.

Objective Wizard: Do not forget the To Do List.

Summary

New Terms

Stream	Disk File
Collection	File Stream
Set Conversion Messages	Data Structure

What Did You Learn?

- Many of the data structure capabilities of Smalltalk are in the `Collection` classes.
- There's a set of criteria for selecting a collection to suit your needs.
- Conversion messages create new kinds of collections from existing ones.
- More can be learned about collections, streams, and disk files in Smalltalk by exploring the message interface to each.

Words of Wisdom

It's usually better to have a collection than to be one. Most of the time it's better to have an instance variable that contains a collection than to be a subclass of a collection, even if it's your only instance variable.

You'll spend much of your implementation time picking and using collections. It pays to learn about them and understand how they work. The best way to learn about collections is to explore the message interfaces and experiment by sending messages to an instance of a collection.

Collection Summary

Collection Comparison Table

Class Name	Indexed	Fixed Size	Duplicates
`Array`	Yes	Yes	Yes
`Bag`	No	No	Yes
`Dictionary`	Yes[1]	No	Yes[1]
`OrderedCollection`	Yes	No	Yes
`Set`	No	No	No
`SortedCollection`[2]	Yes	No	Yes
`String`[3]	Yes	Yes	Yes

1. Instances of `Dictionary` are indexed by any object. The index objects (keys) cannot have duplicates, but the values associated with them can.

2. Instances of `SortedCollection` keep their contents in a sorted order. The sorting is defined by the sort block. The default sort block uses the <= message. The sort block may place restrictions on which objects may be added to a given instance of `SortedCollection`.

3. Instances of `String` can contain only character objects.

Common Message Interface:

`do:`	Repeat a piece of code for each element.
`collect:`	Map each element into a new collection.
`select:`	Filter some elements into a new collection.
`reject:`	Filter an element out; put the rest into a new collection.
`occurrencesOf:`	Answer the number of occurrences of the argument.
`includes:`	Answer true if the argument is in the collection.
`isEmpty`	Answer true if the collection has no elements.
`notEmpty`	Answer true if the collection has elements.
`size`	Answer the number of elements in the collection.

To Do List

Create a class called `Stack`, which implements a normal set of stack operations. For now, make it a subclass of `Object`. The message interface should include the following:

`push: anObject`	Put `anObject` on the top of the stack.
`pop`	Answer the object on top of the stack after removing it.
`size`	Answer the number of elements in the stack.

`isEmpty`	Answer `true` if the stack is empty; else, answer `false`.
`clear`	Clear the stack.

There's a programming trick that initializes the instance variables of an object as soon as it is created. You may find it useful for the `Stack` class. You can find an example in the class method `new` and in the instance method `initialize`. Both are in class `Bag`.

Implement a class called `SalesRecorder`, which supports the entry of sales information. Initially, sales information will be limited to the product sold, but you may wish to make enhancements later. Here is a possible message interface:

`addSale: aProduct`	Add the sale of the product `aProduct`.
`salesOf: aProduct`	Answer the number of sales of `aProduct`.
`totalSales`	Answer the total number of sales.
`clear`	Clear all sales data.

To start, use strings to name your products.

Extra credit: Create a class called `Product`, and integrate it with your sales recorder application.

Keep track of sales by day, week, and month.

10

Booleans and Blocks

Contents at: 'Chapter 10'

#(

boolean
  `true`
  `false`

boolean combinations
boolean comparisons
conditional execution
  `ifTrue: ifFalse:`

blocks

more conditional execution
  `[ ] whileTrue: [ ]`
  `[ ] whileFalse: [ ]`

basic iteration
  `timesRepeat: [ ]`
  `to: do: [:var| ]`
  `to: by: do: [:var| ]`

collection iteration
  `do:`
  `collect:`
  `select:`).

Questions of Interest

- What are Squeak's boolean capabilities?
- What conditional statements can I use?

- What is a Block and how can I use it?
- What iterators are available to me?

Introduction

Much earlier, as we discussed the Smalltalk language, you may have noticed the lack of conditional and iteration constructs. Such constructs were lacking because there are none in the core language. These capabilities are implemented as classes, instances, and methods in the class hierarchy. This implementation has several advantages, not the least of which is that it allows changes in and enhancements of the basic conditional and iteration constructs.

Blocks are the hardest concept to understand in this chapter. You may find it useful to think of a block as a chunk of code that has been stuffed into an object rather than being executed. This stuffing of code allows the code to be executed, more than once if necessary, by sending a message to the block object.

Goals for This Chapter

- To understand the ramifications of the booleans (true and false) being objects.
- To write code using boolean combinations.
- To write code using comparison messages.
- To know and be able to use the available conditional messages.
- To understand the different ways to do iteration in Squeak.
- To understand how to use blocks.

Jim	Objective Wizard
Hi, I'm back yet again.	
	Greetings, human. This time we will be talking about some very important constructs. Are you ready to learn about some additional objects?
Oh? You mean there's more to learn?	
	That, Jim, is an understatement. You have much more to learn. At the moment, I want to discuss how to use booleans, blocks, conditional statements, and iterators in your code.
Yeah, I've been wondering about those.	
	Good, I want to start with booleans. Is your brain booted?
I am a human. My brain does not boot.	
	Yes, I have heard that said about humans...
How are boolean capabilities implemented in Smalltalk?	
	Boolean capabilities in Squeak—as in other Smalltalk systems—are implemented in the abstract class `Boolean` and its subclasses `True` and `False`. The boolean values that we use in our code are instances of `True` and `False`. The instance of `True` can be referenced using the pseudo variable `true`; the instance of `False` can be referenced through the pseudo variable `false`.
Very interesting implementation. How do I combine booleans?	
	The boolean operators *and*, *or*, *not*, *exclusive or*, and *equivalence* are implemented in the classes `Boolean`, `True`, and `False`. Here are the messages used to do these operations:

JIM | OBJECTIVE WIZARD

Operation	Message	Argument
and	&	aBoolean
and	and:	aBlock
or	|	aBoolean
or	or:	aBlock
not	not	none
exclusive or	xor:	aBoolean
equivalence	eqv:	aBoolean

Note that the *and* operation has both a binary message (&) and a keyword message (and:). The binary message always evaluates the code that answers its argument boolean. The keyword message takes an unevaluated piece of code as its argument and does not evaluate it unless it must.

The same holds true for the *or* operation.

JIM: I'm not sure I understand the difference between & and and:. How about an example?

Certainly.

Execute the following piece of code:

```
| x |
x := nil.
x notNil & (x > 0)
   ifFalse: [Smalltalk beep].
```

You will get a "does not understand" error because nil does not handle the > message. (Ah, think of the havoc that would ensue if humans had internal "does not understand" errors.) The code (x > 0) executes because the & message simply takes two boolean values as arguments.

The and: message takes an unevaluated piece of code as an argument and executes it only if necessary. The following piece of code will work correctly:

```
| x |
x := nil.
(x notNil and: [x > 0])
   ifFalse: [Smalltalk beep].
```

JIM	OBJECTIVE WIZARD
	Here the code [x > 0] is never executed, and thus there is no error.
I think I understand. Square brackets make it so that the code doesn't execute right away.	
	Correct. It is called a block. We will discuss blocks in more detail in a future meeting so as not to overwhelm you now.
How do you compare and test objects?	
	You compare and test objects with a comparison message. In Smalltalk, a *comparison message* is any message that answers either `true` or `false`. Here are some common comparison messages:

Operation	Message
equal	=
not equal	~=
greater than	>
less than	<
is odd number	`odd`
is even number	`even`
is the nil object	`isNil`
is not the nil object	`notNil`
exactly equal	==
not exactly equal	~~

Every object either implements or inherits the messages `isNil`, `notNil`, =, ~=, ==, and ~~. These messages will work with any object.

JIM: Well, except for that weird stuff with the pseudo variables `true` and `false`, booleans in Smalltalk are similar to what I'm used to.

JIM | OBJECTIVE WIZARD

What about some conditional statements?

Smalltalk's *conditional statements* are simply messages to a boolean object. The messages are as follows:

```
ifTrue:ifFalse:
ifFalse:ifTrue:
ifTrue:
ifFalse:
```

Notice that these are all the possible combinations of `ifTrue:` and `ifFalse:`. The arguments for all of these messages are zero argument blocks, which are really pieces of code that have not yet been executed.

Does this make sense to you, Jim?

I think I understand everything except that block thing. Some examples would help.

The block thing, as you call it, is implemented in the class `ContextPart` and its subclasses. As you may remember from earlier discussions—although I am discovering that it is just as likely you do not remember—a block is one or more Smalltalk expressions surrounded by brackets `[ ]`. Blocks are used throughout the system, particularly in conditional and iteration statements. Here's an example:

```
(5 odd) ifTrue:
 [SoundPlayer boinkScale]
```

Reading this expression tells us that the `ifTrue:` message was sent to the object returned from the `(5 odd)` expression. In this case, a `true` is returned from `(5 odd)`. As a result, the `ifTrue:` method executes the block of code `[SoundPlayer boinkScale]` by sending the block the `value` message.

Here are more examples:

```
count isNil
   ifTrue: [count := 1]
   ifFalse: [count := count + 1].
```

JIM

OBJECTIVE WIZARD

`ifTrue:ifFalse`, like every other message, returns a value. In this case, the value comes from the piece of code that gets evaluated. The last example above could be rewritten as follows:

```
count :=
   count isNil
      ifTrue: [1]
      ifFalse: [count + 1].
```

The only meaningful difference between them is one of style.

Here is one more example:

```
count > 10000 ifTrue: [
   count := 0.
   list := OrderedCollection new.
^self error: 'Overflow problem'].
```

Okay, I'm sure I understand the testing and conditional execution stuff. I would still like to know more about these blocks.

Blocks come in different flavors based on the number of arguments they take. We will discuss zero-, one-, and two-argument blocks, because they are the most common—tasty, shall we say for your convenience.

A *zero-argument block* is a block with no variables declared in the block. The `SoundPlayer boinkScale` example shown earlier uses a zero-argument block. Many of the conditional and iteration messages in Smalltalk use zero-argument blocks. For example:

```
x odd
   ifTrue: ['I''m odd']
   ifFalse: ['I''m even'].

| counter |
counter := 0.
[counter < 100] whileTrue: [
   counter := counter + 1.
   Smalltalk beep.]
```

JIM | OBJECTIVE WIZARD

Jim: Whoa, wait a picosecond! What is the `whileTrue:` message all about?

Objective Wizard: They are looping messages that can be sent to zero-argument blocks. Each `whileTrue:` and `whileFalse:` message will iteratively execute the code in its argument as long as the receiver object returns the boolean that it requires in order to continue.

Simple, yes?

Jim: Yeah.

Objective Wizard: Another looping construct uses the `timesRepeat:` message and is implemented in class `Integer`. When sent to an integer, it executes its argument—a zero-argument block—the integer number of times. For example, look at the following code:

```
10 timesRepeat:[SoundPlayer boinkScale].
```

Jim: I was wondering how iteration would be implemented. I'm glad we finally got to it.

Objective Wizard: There is more iteration to come in later discussions, but for now let us continue with the next flavor of block.

A *one-argument block* takes, as you would expect, one object as an argument. The variable used is declared at the front of the block. One-argument blocks are used in some iteration statements.

The `to:do:` message lets you iterate over a range of numbers.

```
| array |
array := Array new: 20.
1 to: 20 do: [:index |
   array at: index
         put: index factorial].
```

```
| total |
total := 1.
1 to: 100 do: [:integer |
   total := total * integer].
```

JIM

The last time we met, you said you would tell me about some iteration messages for collections.

OBJECTIVE WIZARD

Yes, I did, and now is as good a time as any, which is often the case in dealing with humans.

Look in class `Collection`, and you will see the following iteration messages:

```
do:
collect:
select:
reject:
```

Each of these messages takes a one-argument block as an argument and executes the block for each element in the collection. The `collect:`, `select:`, and `reject:` messages also answer the new collection that is built on the basis of the collection that received the given message.

The `collect:` message maps the contents of the receiver collection to another collection of the same size. Each element in the new collection is mapped using the block to the new collection. For example,

```
#(1 9 4) collect:
   [:num | num squared].
```

answers the collection `#(1 81 16).` Note that it answers a collection of elements that have changed according to the code in the block.

The `select:` message picks particular elements from the receiver collection to put into another collection. The selection is done by the block. If it answers `true`, the element is added to the new collection; if it answers `false`, it is not added. Here's an example:

```
#(1 9 4 7) select:
   [:num | num > 5].
```

This example answers the collection `#(9 7).`

JIM | OBJECTIVE WIZARD

The `reject:` message works like `select:` but answers a collection of elements for which the block evaluates to `false`. The code fragment

```
#(1 9 4 7) reject:
   [:num | num > 5].
```

answers the collection `#(1 4)`.

This is more than I expected. Blocks are great!

Hold on, Jim. There is more.

A *two-argument block* takes two objects as arguments. The variables used are declared at the front of the block. Two argument blocks are used for sort blocks and `inject: into:` messages.

The `inject:into:` message can be used to summarize the information in a collection. The message takes a starting point and a two-argument block that combines elements as its arguments. The following statement sums all the numbers in the collection:

```
#(1 2 99 5)
inject: 0
into: [:sofar :num | sofar + num].
```

This example answers the number `107`.

The capabilities of `inject:into:` are not limited to adding a bunch of numbers. Here is another, slightly more complex example:

```
#('I' 'like' 'Squeak')
   inject: (String new)
   into: [:sentence :word |
      sentence ,
         (String with: Space),
         word].
```

This example answers the string `'I like Squeak'`.

Wow! Blocks really pack a wallop!

Jim	Objective Wizard
	Right (...yawn). Excuse my lack of human excitability over such matters. Move on now—go implement the To Do List.
I'm looking forward to it.	
	I am sure you are. In the meantime, I will get some rest before our next discussion. See you later.

Summary

New Terms

Block	Iteration Message
Boolean	Comparison Message

What Did You Learn?

- How to reference the boolean values `true` and `false`.
- How to create booleans using comparison messages.
- How to do conditional execution with the `ifTrue:ifFalse:` messages.
- How to use the `whileTrue:` and other basic iteration messages.
- How to iterate over collections in several different ways.

Words of Wisdom

There is nothing magical about a block. It's an object and so can be assigned to variables, passed as arguments, and sent messages. You can even add new messages to its message interface. Here's an example of assigning a variable to a block:

```
| code |
code := [Smalltalk beep].
3 timesRepeat: code.
```

This code may look strange, but it works just fine.

If you don't like it, fix it. Most of Squeak is written in itself, with the source code available. This set-up gives you this wonderful capability but makes it hard to complain.

To Do List

Recall that blocks are implemented in the class `ContextPart` and its subclasses. Spend some time looking at the message interface to these subclasses. Pay special attention to the `value`, `value:` and `value:value:` methods. Also, look at the message interface for the classes `True` and `False`. Look closely at the `ifTrue:ifFalse:` messages and how they are implemented.

Use the following code to generate an array of some class names:

```
A:= (ProtoObject allSubclasses
   Select: [c|
      (c name at: 2) = $e])
   asArray
```

Write code that iterates through this list and prints all the class names that end in "r" onto the transcript. Try to do this task another way. What's the shortest piece of code you can write to accomplish this task?

Use the file list browser to create a text file with several lines of text in it. (*Hint:* The yellow-button submenu—produced by doing a yellow-button click in the upper right pane—contains the menu item **add new file**. Enter your text in the lower pane.) Open a Workspace, and write code that will count the number of each kind of character in the file (ignoring case). After you have the code working, add more code to print the results of the count onto the Transcript window. The report should be in ASCII order.

The Transcript window can be accessed by sending messages to the global variable `Transcript`. Some messages that the Transcript can handle are `nextPut:`, `nextPutAll:`, and `.cr`.

When writing the code, don't try to find the fastest or shortest code; instead, go for the simplest. In this case, simplest means the easiest to write.

11

More Blocks

Contents at: 'Chapter 11'

#(

Other Control Structures
  `ifNil:ifNotNil:`
  repeat
  Collection iteration

Background Processes

Error Handling
  `ifError:`
  Exception System
  Specialized Error Handlers).

Questions of Interest

- What control structures does Smalltalk have?
- How can background processes be started?
- What is a thread of execution?
- In what ways are errors detected and handled?

Introduction

In Chapter 10, "Booleans and Blocks," the use of blocks to implement basic control structures such as if-then-else, while loops, and collection iteration was introduced. This chapter expands beyond that basic understanding of blocks to show a wider range of uses of blocks in controlling the flow of execution in both simple and sophisticated ways. This expansion includes special purpose control structures, exception handling, and how to start background processes.

Because blocks—like everything else in Squeak—are objects, these control structures using blocks are implemented as part of the same class library that implements the rest of the Squeak environment. Also, because the classes can be modified and extended, the set of control structures can be modified and extended. Thus, the list of control structures available in the Squeak environment may change as a result of new versions of the image, additions by applications, changes in libraries, and hacks by you.

Goals for This Chapter

- To learn some of the more advanced control structures available in the Squeak environment.
- To be able to create simple background processes.
- To be able to write code that captures and handles error conditions.
- To understand ways that blocks can be used to create new control structures.

JIM

OBJECTIVE WIZARD

Jim: Yo, Wiz.

Wizard: Hello, Jim. It is good to see you again. What can I do for you?

Jim: I was looking at a few fragments of Smalltalk code someone sent me when I noticed the following code:

```
^x ifNil: [0].
```

Wizard: Yes?

Jim: What does it do?

Wizard: If the variable `x` is `nil`, then it returns zero; otherwise, it returns the value of `x`.

Jim: It has square brackets. Doesn't that mean it's a control structure? I don't remember it from when we talked about ifs and loops.

Wizard: Yes and no. Remember that blocks are just another kind of object. Control structures in Smalltalk are no different from other kinds of methods. The `ifNil:` message is one of a number of special purpose control structures that have been implemented in Squeak.

Jim: You did say that blocks were just another kind of object, but this still seems weird.

What are some of the other special purpose control structures?

Wizard: There are many special purpose methods that act like control structures. For example, there are several variations of the `ifNil:` message, just as there are variations of the `ifTrue:` message:

```
ifNil:
ifNotNil:
ifNil:ifNotNil
ifNotNil:ifNil:
```

JIM | OBJECTIVE WIZARD

Jim: How would `ifNotNil:` be useful?

Objective Wizard: The `nil` object is often used to mark undefined values. Often special processing should be applied to undefined values, as in the `ifNil:` example you found. Other times, there should be something done if the value is not undefined, such as in the following method:

```
lookupAddress
      "Answer an address"
   ^id ifNotNil: [table at: id].
```

Jim: And the `ifNil:ifNotNil:` message is for when you want to do both?

Objective Wizard: Yes. My, my, you seem to be plugging right along.

Jim: So, what other messages are there?

Objective Wizard: There are variations of the `whileTrue:` message. For example,

```
[Smalltalk beep.
 (Delay forSeconds: 1) wait.
] repeat.
```

will cause the system to beep once per second until it is interrupted. Quite harmonious to my ear.

Jim: An infinite loop.

Objective Wizard: Yes, unless you escape using a return.

There are also unary messages—`whileTrue` and `whileFalse`—that do not take a block of code as an argument. They are useful when the test condition is at the end of a piece of code.

Jim: Those messages might be useful sometimes, although you could do all that using normal while messages.

JIM | OBJECTIVE WIZARD

That is exactly right. They are used to write shorter or more easily understood code, but they are not necessary. Humans, especially, tend to like things short and easy, but these qualities are not necessary.

Are there more messages?

Most iteration is done over a collection. There are several messages we have not yet discussed for iterating over the elements in a collection. The contents of a collection can be searched for an element that meets a particular condition, as follows:

```
#(1 3 4 5 8 9)
   detect: [:n | n even]
```

This example will return the integer 4, since that is the first even-numbered element of the list.

What if there wasn't an even number in the list? Would it return `nil`?

No, it would signal an error. To return `nil`, you would do the following:

```
#(1 3 5 7 9)
   detect: [:n | n even]
   ifNone: [nil].
```

This variation executes the second block if none of the elements in the collection makes the first block evaluate to `true`.

So, if it doesn't find anything in the list that fits the first block, then it does the default action after `ifNone:`.

An informal but accurate description.

Another collection iterator is a message that tests to see if every element in a list meets a condition.

```
#(1 3 5 7)
   allSatisfy: [:n | n odd].

#(1 3 4 7)
   allSatisfy: [:n | n odd].
```

JIM | OBJECTIVE WIZARD

Objective Wizard: The first expression will return `true` because all the numbers in the array are odd. The second will return `false` because 4 is not odd.

Jim: This is pretty cool. I knew blocks were powerful—and used for conditionals and loops—but I didn't realize you could do so much with them.

Objective Wizard: As usual, there is even more. Another way to use blocks to handle control flow is to create background processes.

Jim: What's a background process?

Objective Wizard: It is a separate thread of execution, a way to execute several pieces of code at one time. One way this thread is used is to do something that may take a long time to execute. Humans, as you should know, are not patient creatures. If

```
10 timesRepeat: [
   (Delay forSeconds: 6) wait.
   Smalltalk beep].
```

is typed into a Workspace and then executed, you will not be able to use the Squeak user interface until it is done executing.

However,

```
[10 timesRepeat: [
   (Delay forSeconds: 6) wait.
   Smalltalk beep]] fork.
```

will execute in a background process and, therefore, you may continue using the system while it happens.

Jim: These threads sound like the threads supported in some other languages.

Objective Wizard: That is true, although the underlying implementation may be different. Be careful not to simplify these matters by relying on your experience prior to our discussions here in ObjectLand.

JIM	OBJECTIVE WIZARD
So how many background processes can you have running?	
	You may have as many background processes running as memory and processor speed limitations allow. Processes at the same priority will take turns. Processes with higher priorities will be given time before processes with lower priorities.
Priorities?	
	Priorities define layers of processes, with the top layers always given time before the lower layers. Perhaps it is akin to your human concept of organizing tasks into an efficient sequence.
Like vacuuming before dusting?	
	I am unfamiliar with such terms. There is a set of messages you can send to the Global variable `Processor` to access these priorities. Unless you are doing systems programming, you will typically use only the user background priority, which is the one used by the `fork` message.
I don't think I understand what that means.	
	That means, use the `fork` message until you are sure you need more control.
That I understand.	
	Do you want to know anything else?
How about a switch or case statement?	
	There is none.
Really?	
	Yes, but you may build one if you wish. In fact, I will add it to your To Do List.
Thanks, I think.	

JIM | OBJECTIVE WIZARD

Hey, what about exceptions? Those are a kind of control-flow construct.

That is true. There are a number of ways to capture and deal with errors in Squeak. First, let us cause an error:

```
#(1 2 4) at: 5.
```

When executed, this code will cause an error, because 5 is outside the bounds of the array. One way to capture such an error is to wrap it in a block and use the `ifError:` message:

```
[#(1 2 4) at: 5]
   ifError: [:msg :obj | nil].
```

The argument to this message is a two-argument block whose first argument will be the string that represents the error and whose second argument will be the object that receives the message. The expression as a whole will return whatever value is returned by the argument block if an error occurs, or by the receiver block if the expression executes normally.

How about another example?

Very well.

Another error that can occur is dividing by zero. The following code will cause a division by zero to return the floating point representation for infinity when there is an error in the division:

```
| x |
x := 0.
[1 / x] ifError: [:msg :obj |
   Float infinity]
```

This code would be more appropriate if we could be sure the error was caused by a zero value in the denominator rather than by some other problem. More control is available using another error-handling system based on exception objects. The code above can then be written specifically for a divide-by-zero error, as follows:

JIM | OBJECTIVE WIZARD

```
| x |
x := 0.
[1 / x]
   on: ZeroDivide
   do: [Float infinity].
```

So, I can use either system to handle an error?

Yes, although errors designed for the first system are all grouped under the exception `Error`.

Can I create new kinds of exceptions?

Of course. Types of exceptions are represented as classes. New exception types can be added by creating new subclasses of `Exception` or of one of its existing subclasses.

So, these two techniques are how errors are handled in Smalltalk code?

That is not exactly the case. Most common errors are handled by messages that allow an error handler to be specified directly. An example is the `'detect:ifNone'` message I mentioned earlier. The block specified with the `'ifNone:'` keyword is used when a common error condition occurs—in this case, the error condition that no such object can be found in the collection.

What other messages like this are there?

There are many. Try using the Method Finder tool with the keywords `ifAbsent:` and `ifNone:`. One example is the array access error we just used.

```
[#(1 2 4) at: 5]
   ifError: [:msg :obj | nil].
```

The same effect could be achieved using the `at: ifAbsent:` message:

```
#(1 2 4) at: 5 ifAbsent: [nil].
```

JIM | OBJECTIVE WIZARD

Jim: This is a lot of new stuff!

Objective Wizard: And there is more. Blocks allow Smalltalk considerable freedom in constructing specialized control structures, and Squeak takes advantage of that capability. However, we have covered the most important uses, and, clearly, you can handle little more at this juncture.

Jim: Guess I better head back then. See you later, Wiz.

Objective Wizard: Good-bye.

Summary

New Terms

Thread

Exception

Background Process

What Did You Learn?

- How to use some additional control structures.
- How to create background processes.
- Several ways of dealing with errors in Smalltalk code.
- How to use the exception system.

Words of Wisdom

Some messages, such as the `at:ifAbsent:` message, have variations that allow a block to be specified for exception situations, while others do not. You will find that the messages that do have these variations are those that often have exception conditions. If you are often wrapping a particular message in an error block, it can be a good idea to write your own method that uses a special purpose exception block.

Computers are cheaper than programmers, and so you should rarely worry about optimization. Sometimes you must, however, and when that happens you should know that Smalltalk compilers have special knowledge about some of the most basic control structure messages such as the `ifTrue:` message and the `whileTrue:` and `whileFalse:` messages. These messages can be compiled more compactly and efficiently than the special purpose control structures.

To Do List

Add a new method called `ifEq:do:` to the class `Object`. It should take an object as the first argument and a block as the second argument. If the receiver is equal to the first argument, then the block should be executed.

The following message can be used to implement a simple form of case statement:

```
(FillInTheBlankMorph request: 'What color?')
   ifEq: 'red' do: [^Color red];
   ifEq: 'green' do: [^Color green];
   ifEq: 'blue' do: [^Color lightBlue].
```

What are the limitations of this implementation? How could it be fixed? (*Hint:* You may need to create a new class).

Create a new version of the binary divide message in Number called `div:ifDenomZero:`, which takes a block as its second argument so it can be used as follows:

```
| x |
x := 0.
1 div: x ifDenomZero: [Float infinity].
```

This exercise can be done instead of using an `ifError:` or `on:do:` message to capture the zero-divide exception.

In a Workspace, write a piece of code that will beep on the hour. Then, wrap it in a block. Before sending it the `fork` message, think about how you would stop the code from executing if you got tired of it. (*Hint:* One way to do this is to use a Global variable as a flag.)

12

Files and Streams

Contents at: 'Chapter 12'

#(

Questions of Interest

- How are text files manipulated in Squeak?
- How can nonstring objects be written and read to a file?
- Can streams be used without a file?
- How can directories and folders be used?

Introduction

Squeak, like many other programming systems, uses streams to read and write information to and from files. Smalltalk differs from most languages in two ways. First, the stream and file interface is represented as objects. Second, streams can be used to read and write objects as well as bytes, characters, and strings. The ability to read and write objects eliminates most of the problems associated with creating and maintaining a file format for your data. This ability can also be used as a way to read and write objects over a communication channel for network or Web applications.

Streams are very useful tools in a variety of situations beyond reading and writing files. One of their most important uses is to interpret and generate formatted text. If you are unfamiliar with this idea, you may want to spend some time looking at how messages such as `nextPutAll:` and `upTo:` are used by classes in the Squeak environment.

Goals for This Chapter

- To know how to open, close, read from, and write to text files.
- To know how to read and write objects to a file.
- To understand the use of `FileDirectory` to manipulate directories and folders.
- To get some idea of the uses of streams outside of reading and writing files.

JIM	OBJECTIVE WIZARD
Hello? Is anyone home?	
	Jim, it is nice to see you again.
I have a question, if you've got some time.	
	Certainly, with what can I help you?
I have to write a script that translates a file generated by an old Fortran program into a form that can be imported into a spreadsheet. It's easy to do, so I thought I would try to write it in Smalltalk.	
	That is an excellent idea. Since you already understand the problem, you will be able to concentrate on learning the tool.
That's the idea. The problem is that I don't know how to handle text files in Smalltalk.	
	You should have no difficulties. Smalltalk uses a stream-based system with which you are probably familiar from your experience using other programming languages. Streams are a way of looking at a collection in which you can see only one object at a time. Reading from or writing to a stream shifts the object you can see to the next one in the collection.
We've talked about streams before.	
	That is right, but it never hurts to repeat a little. Streams in the Squeak environment are built around a set of classes whose superclass is `Stream`.

JIM	OBJECTIVE WIZARD

```
Stream
   DataStream
      ReferenceStream
         SmartRefStream
      PositionableStream
         ReadStream
         WriteStream
            ReadWriteStream
               FileStream
```

There are also classes that either implement versions of these streams or are designed for specific situations.

Jim: Umm...what's a `SmartRefStream`? What—no answer, Wiz?

`DataStream` and its subclasses are streams designed for reading and writing arbitrary objects rather than characters or bytes. Since your problem involves text files, let us start with file streams.

Jim: Okay.

To work with files, there is one more class with which you must be familiar, `FileDirectory`, which represents a directory or folder.

Jim: But how do I use these classes to do stuff like opening a file?

If you know the name of a file, you can open it with the following code:

```
FileStream fileNamed:
   'somefile.txt'.
```

This code fragment returns an instance of `FileStream`, which can be used to read and write the contents of the file.

Jim: So, how would I read the contents?

There are a number of different messages you can use to read the contents of a file. The `next` message will read a sin-

JIM | OBJECTIVE WIZARD

gle character. The `nextLine` message will read a line of text. The `upTo:` message will read until a particular character is found. There are also many other messages.

Okay, the `readLine` looks really useful for this problem. Or maybe `upTo:`, since the data in the file is comma delimited. Could you help me construct some code?

Certainly. Tell me what you need, and I will write the code that does it.

Right. First, I need to open one file to read from, say `DA20115.DTA`, and another one to write the modified data, say `15Jan2002.txt`.

I will generate an instance of `FileStream` for each file and store them in Workspace variables.

```
inStream:= FileStream
   fileNamed: 'DA20115.DTA'.
outStream:= FileStream
   newFileNamed: '15Jan2002.txt'.
```

What does `newFileNamed:` do?

It ensures that the file does not already exist and, if it does exist, gives the user a warning.

Oh, that's a nice touch.

Now I need to go through the contents of the input file, read in a line at a time, and then break the line into fields and write them to the output file with tabs instead of commas.

That is a bit much all at once. I will start by writing code that reads lines from the input.

JIM	OBJECTIVE WIZARD

```
[inStream atEnd] whileFalse: [
   line := inStream nextLine.
   ].
```

JIM: That's easy enough. Now, how do I break up the line into fields?

OBJECTIVE WIZARD: There are several ways to accomplish that. Since we are talking about streams here, let us use a solution that makes use of streams. Given a line of text from the input file, the following code will iterate through the comma-delimited fields in that line:

```
lStream := ReadStream
   on: line.
[lStream atEnd] whileFalse: [
   field := lStream upTo: $,.
   ].
```

Note that a stream over the line of text is created using the `on:` message. This process works for any indexable collection, not just for strings.

JIM: So, you turn each line into a stream and use `upTo:` to read the individual fields? Does that mean you create a new file for each line?

OBJECTIVE WIZARD: No, Jim. Streams do not have to be connected to files. The `on:` message will create a stream over the contents of any indexed collection.

JIM: That's handy. Now, how do we write the data to the new stream?

OBJECTIVE WIZARD: By using the `nextPutAll:`, `tab`, and `cr` messages. I think we are ready to put the pieces together and add the code to write to the file.

JIM / OBJECTIVE WIZARD

```
in := FileStream
   fileNamed: 'DA20115.DTA'.
out := FileStream
   newFileNamed: '15Jan2002.txt'.
[inStream atEnd] whileFalse: [
   line := inStream nextLine.
   lStream := ReadStream
      on: line.
   [lStream atEnd] whileFalse: [
      field := lStream upTo: $,.
      outStream nextPutAll:
            field.
      outStream tab.
      ].
   outStream cr.
   ].
```

Hmm...I think I see what's going on. Hey! What about closing the files?

You are correct; files should always be closed after use. Put the following at the end of the code:

```
inStream close.
outStream close.
```

Also, note that we used several Workspace variables to reference the file streams and the line and field values. That approach is fine for one-off programming in a Workspace, but those variables must be declared as instance or local variables if the code is placed in a method.

Of course.

Is there anything else you want to know?

Yes, I wanted to know more about that DataStream stuff—but before we do that, could you help me write another piece of file code?

Yes, what would you like to do?

JIM

OBJECTIVE WIZARD

Jim: I need to do some clean-up work and file management. Once I've converted the files, I want to delete the old ones. I also want to convert all the files in a directory without having to do them one at a time.

Objective Wizard: You need to use the `FileDirectory` class I mentioned earlier. It represents a directory or folder and contains many messages for managing files and other directories.

Instances of `FileDirectory` can be created using the `default` message, which returns the current default directory, or by using the `on:` message, which creates a directory based on a pathname. Optionally, once you have a directory, there are messages for accessing the parent directory and for creating and accessing subdirectories.

Jim: That last part sounds like what I need. I can dump all the files into my Squeak directory. How do I work with a subdirectory named `Jan2002`?

Objective Wizard: To create a subdirectory, use the following code:

```
FileDirectory default
   createDirectory: 'Jan2002'.
```

To create a `FileDirectory` instance for a subdirectory like the one we just created, use the following code:

```
dir := FileDirectory default
   directoryNamed: 'Jan2002'.
```

To get a list of all the names in the directory, use the following code:

```
dir fileNames.
```

To delete a directory, use the following code:

```
FileDirectory default
   deleteDirectory: 'Jan2002'.
```

JIM

OBJECTIVE WIZARD

That one that gets files in a directory sounds like just what I need. Can I just use `fileNames` and one of the file iterators—maybe `do:`—to go through the names of the files in a directory?

Yes, that would work. Use something like the following:

```
| dir fs |
dir := FileDirectory default
   directoryNamed: 'Jan2002'.
dir fileNames do: [:fname |
   fs := dir fileNamed: fname.
   "Do file work here"
   fs close.
   ].
```

Great. That will save me a lot of time.

Is there anything else today?

I still want to hear about `SmartRefStream`.

Very well, but that is all for today. I do not want your brain to get too full.

Okay, good thinking.

A `DataStream` is a stream that converts objects into a form that can be stored and retrieved. It is actually a translator that contains a character stream and flattens objects into a form that can be written to such a stream. Not a pleasant experience, but sometimes necessary.

You've been written to `DataStream`?

I would rather not talk about it.

Oh, well sure.

JIM	OBJECTIVE WIZARD
	The problem with a `DataStream` is that it reads and writes objects, and any objects referenced by those objects, without really paying attention to the contents.
Why is that a problem?	
	Objects are not simple characters or records. They can contain references to themselves, references to classes, or multiple references to the same object. If that is the case, then a `ReferenceStream` should be used instead. It keeps track of which objects it has written or read so that each object needs to be stored only once. If an object is written or read multiple times, a reference is used instead, hence the name.
Then what does a `SmartRefStream` do?	
	A `SmartRefStream` is used when you think that the structure of the objects might change, as often happens when a system is being developed. It remembers the structure and knows that it must use a conversion message if things change.
That *is* pretty smart. How are these things used?	
	Much like an ordinary stream. The message `next` returns the next object from the stream, and `nextPut:` writes an object. The `close` message is used to close the stream, if that is necessary. Of course, there are other messages that may be useful, but I have revealed the basics.
So, if I had a collection of objects and I wanted to save them to a file, how would I do it?	
	First, you would decide which type of stream to use. In general, I would recommend a `ReferenceStream`. If the collection were in the global variable `MyCollection`, you could write it to the file `saved` with the following code:

```
(ReferenceStream newFileNamed:
      'saved')
   nextPutAll: MyCollection;
   close.
```

JIM | OBJECTIVE WIZARD

That code would write each of the objects to the file. You could also save the collection object by changing `nextPutAll:` to `nextPut:`.

```
(ReferenceStream newFileNamed:
      'saved2')
   nextPut: MyCollection;
   close.
```

Huh?

Remember that the collection is an object, too. You can save the object that is the collection, rather than saving each of the individual objects in the collection.

Oh, I see. So, if the collection had five objects, the first way would be to write five objects in the file, and the second way would be to write a single object that was the collection of five objects.

Yes. The advantage of the second technique can be seen in the way it is read back in. Writing individual objects would require that they be read one at a time, as follows:

```
| rs |
MyCollection :=
   OrderedCollection new.
rs := ReferenceStream fileNamed:
   'saved'.
[rs atEnd] whileFalse: [
   MyCollection add: rs next].
rs close.
```

However, writing the entire collection as a single object would allow you to load the objects with the following code:

```
|  rs |
rs := ReferenceStream fileNamed:
   'saved2'.
MyCollection := rs next.
rs close.
```

JIM / OBJECTIVE WIZARD

Jim: That *is* easier, although the first technique is more flexible. Anything else I should know?

Objective Wizard: Several things. To set a stream back to its beginning so it can be reread or overwritten, use the `reset` message. To position a character stream at a particular place, use `position:`. To open an interactive file dialog use `StandardFileMenu`.

Jim: How do you use that?

Objective Wizard: There are class methods in `StandardFileMenu` for getting existing files or for creating new ones. They come in different varieties for different tasks. Here is a simple example:

```
result :=
   StandardFileMenu oldFile.
```

This code will return an object that you can use to access the file name and directory chosen by the user. If no file is chosen, the result will be `nil`.

Jim: What kind of object does it return?

Objective Wizard: That is for you to find out. Check the To Do List.

Jim: Anything else, or are you sending me off?

Objective Wizard: Squeak is large. There is always more. However, this is enough for now. Ciao.

Jim: Thanks. See you around.

Summary

New Terms

FileStream	DataStream
FileDirectory	ReferenceStream

What Did You Learn?

- How to open and close files.
- How to manage files and directories using `FileDirectory`.
- Basic messages for accessing the contents of streams such as `next`, `nextPut:`, and `nextPutAll:`.
- Messages for working with lines in a text stream such as `nextLine` and `cr`.
- How to write and read objects to and from a file.

Words of Wisdom

Watch out for terminology. For example, the entity into which files are organized is called a directory on some systems, is called a folder in others, and is represented in Squeak by the class `FileDirectory`. Because Squeak is a portable system, it will make choices about terminology either by choosing the terms from one system or by inventing its own.

The world is filled with text files. Smalltalk includes many methods that will help you manage them. Check what is available in `Stream`, `ReadStream`, and `ReadWriteStream` before trying to do it yourself.

To Do List

Jim messed up. He deleted the old files he was converting from but then found out that he had made a minor mistake and had to retranslate them. While he reloads the files from magnetic tape (it's a very old system), think about alternatives to deleting the files. Write code fragments that implement those alternatives. (*Hint:* Look at the messages implemented by `FileDirectory`.)

Write code that, given a class, writes a report to a file that includes the name of the class as well as a list of the messages that the class implements, indented with a tab under the class name.

You can get a tab character by sending the `tab` message to the `Character` class. You can get a list of the messages that a class implements using the `selectors` message, and the name of a class can be retrieved using the `name` message.

Now, modify the code to accept a list of classes and a file name to write the report to.

Create a list of `Point` objects using the following code:

```
points := (1 to: 10) with: (10 to: 1 by: -1) collect: [:x :y | x@y].
```

Now, write the `point` objects to a file. There are three ways to do this task. The easiest way is to write the entire collection of points using a `ReferenceStream`. The next easiest way is to write each individual point. The hardest way is to develop a file format and write the points as a binary or text file. Try more than one way.

Now write the matching code to reread the file.

Part III

Advanced ObjectLand

13

Object-Oriented Thinking and Design

Contents at: 'Chapter 13'

#(

Object-Oriented Thinking (OOT)
  OO thinking means thinking in O's
  OO thinking tools
    metaphor
    visualization
    animation
    anthropomorphism
    perspective

Object-Oriented Design (OOD)
  prolonged OOT
  assisted by a methodology
  focused on a particular goal

  An OOD methodology:
    state the problem
    visualize it
    animate it
    identify classes
    describe object states
    list message interfaces
    implement the methods).

Questions of Interest

- What is the object-oriented paradigm?
- How can I make the shift?

Introduction

By this point, you have gained a good understanding of the object-oriented programming paradigm, a little about how to think in terms of objects as computational entities, and a bit about how to design software using objects and messages. The purpose of this chapter is to discuss in more detail the nature of the object-oriented paradigm.

Much attention has been focused on the notion of the object-oriented paradigm. The bulk of this discussion has centered around the objects that make up the implementation, but little instruction has been devoted to how the objects get selected and created by the designer. While the OO paradigm is about objects and messages, it is also about a new sort of problem solving, a style that uses objects as the fundamental units of expression for the solution. This new manner of problem solving requires a new mode of thinking and a new set of thinking tools. This shift is the essence of the object-oriented paradigm.

The information in this chapter is only an introduction to material that could fill another entire book. Use this information now; you will be able to learn more about it later.

Goals for This Chapter

- To think about the real world in terms of objects and messages.
- To find an effective path from the problem specification level to the object-oriented design level.
- When you are finished with this chapter, you will have designed three different applications from the To Do List and, perhaps more importantly, you will have an object-oriented design representation of a project of interest to you.

JIM	OBJECTIVE WIZARD
Hi! I'm back.	
	Hello, Jim. How are your software development activities coming along?
Hmm, I understand the concepts, the language, and parts of the class hierarchy. I can also write Smalltalk code in the Squeak environment. But I keep thinking in terms of data and structure. I have this recurring urge to construct a dataflow chart of my software. I'm also having major difficulty with designing software in this paradigm.	
	Jim, look deep into my implementation. What do you see?
I see variables, dataflow, control flow, and some other stuff.	
	Jim, my procedural friend, you have not yet shifted your paradigm.
How can you tell that?	
	You are still viewing software from the point of view of software abstractions—that is, data, control, and structure.
What? You mean after all this work I still don't understand this paradigm?	
	No. I suspect you understand as much as you need to understand, but you are missing the knowledge and skill necessary to apply what you understand.
So, how should I view software in the OO paradigm?	
	When we write software here in ObjectLand, we look to the problem domain for descriptions of the solution. We design in terms of objects, state, and behavior as we see them in the

JIM	OBJECTIVE WIZARD
	problem domain. We describe the elements of our software in the domain vocabulary. We use the abstractions of the ProblemWorld, not the abstractions of the software domain. Have you noticed that all software in, let us say, the procedural paradigm is expressed in terms of abstractions that have meaning only within the computing world?
Yeah...	
	Here in ObjectLand we do not think in terms of ComputerLand abstractions. We recognize that there is a ComputerLand somewhere deep in each of us. But we also have evolved to the point at which we realize that there is a more expressive, simple, and accurate way of describing the ProblemWorld. That better way makes use of terms and abstractions that actually exist in the ProblemWorld.
Sounds as if what I need is a lesson in object-oriented thinking.	
	Yes. The real shift in paradigm is the shift that takes place in your mind. Object-oriented thinking (OOT) is the essence of the object-oriented paradigm.
What are the components of the paradigm shift?	
	There are four essential components of the object-oriented paradigm shift. You may find more after a while, but you need to accept these four before you can move on in the new paradigm: 1. Objects, messages, and methods are the building blocks of your solution. 2. Look to the problem for the solution and express the solution in the vocabulary of the problem domain. 3. Think in terms of modeling real-world objects. 4. Apply a set of thinking tools to the ProblemWorld in order to create the SolutionWorld.

JIM	OBJECTIVE WIZARD
What do these thinking tools look like?	
	They are tools that we use every day when we operate in the real world. The tools that I will tell you about are as follows: metaphor visualization animation anthropomorphism perspective There are more tools that you will invent as you grow as an object-oriented thinker.
All right, let's talk about metaphor!	
	A *metaphor* is an object that, despite differences, is like another object. Using a metaphor involves the process of substituting one type of object in place of another to suggest or benefit from any likeness or analogy that exists between them.
So what! That's like something from high school English class. How will my using metaphors help me to design?	
	Think about it, Jim. In the object-oriented paradigm, you are actually modeling a real-world object or idea in ObjectLand. Your ability to create that model effectively is strongly related to your knowledge of the real-world object that you are attempting to model. If you can create an intermediate object—a metaphorical object—in your design space, you will have effectively acquired more information about the real-world object. You will have added your knowledge of the metaphorical object to your knowledge of the real-world object you are trying to model. By thinking in terms of metaphors for the problem you are trying to find, you will become a better solution finder.

JIM	OBJECTIVE WIZARD
How about an example?	
	Okay. Imagine that your application is an object used to request information from somewhere on a computer network.
	A metaphor you might use is one of those tear-out cards that you can still find in some magazines. If you have a magazine close at hand, page through it and rip out one of those subscription cards. I will do the same.
Oh yeah, fall-out cards. I thought they were bookmarks that the magazines provide so I can mark articles.	
	What do you see on the card?
	What information does it request?
	How does it behave?
	Well, the one I am holding requests that I write my name and address, check off some subscription information, specify the form in which I will pay, and mail the card. If I accept this metaphor as reasonable for this application, which I do, the implication is that the information the object needs is as follows:
	where to send the information a choice of subscription length what form the payment will take
	The behavior this object should exhibit is the following:
	choosing the subscription length transmitting the request
	The "where to send the information" could be automated by using the address label from the magazine that you subscribe to, or it could be overridden by writing in a different address.
Thinking in terms of metaphors does seem to help me create	

JIM	OBJECTIVE WIZARD
solutions. It almost seems that the metaphor itself is the solution.	
	Sometimes, yes. But usually the metaphor is an intermediate representation of the solution. A metaphor is a convenience with which to work during a design activity and also provides a good intermediate representation to which one can apply additional object-oriented thinking tools. For example, let us apply visualization to our metaphor object.
Wait. I want to know more about visualization before we attempt any integration with my metaphor.	
	Certainly. As a human, you have a tremendous number of cortical neurons associated with visualization. As an object-oriented problem solver using visualization to examine your metaphorical object, you can bring much of your "wetware" on-line to give you additional insights into your solution space.
Sounds good, but how do I use it?	
	A common human activity, particularly for programmers (or so I have heard), is dreaming while awake. You call these waking dreams "daydreams." During these daydreams, you visualize something that you have enjoyed or would like to do. Your daydreams are very visual, are they not?
Yes, they certainly are! I have even daydreamed about the Objective Librarian.	
	In ObjectLand, what you call "daydreaming" we call "visualization of objects of interest." The process is the same. If you can daydream, you can visualize. If you can visualize, you can "see" aspects of objects in much more detail and, consequently, implement them more completely. Try it; you will like it. And it will make you a better object-oriented designer.

JIM	OBJECTIVE WIZARD
Wow, designing can be fun! Give me an example!	
	All right. Begin with a pen. Close your eyes and visualize the various characteristics of the pen. Next, try to visualize the use of the pen. What do you see? What color and size is the nib? What is the pen doing?
Is this related to the `Pen` class we designed earlier, designed conceptually?	
	Sort of, Jim, but stay in the moment here. Sometimes a pen is just a pen. Concern yourself with visualizing the real-world object.
So, visualizing my metaphorical object actually provides a clearer understanding of the solution?	
	Very good! Notice that you are looking to the problem to find the solution. You are becoming an OO thinker.
What's next?	
	Try animating the object you are visualizing. Make the animated object behave in the manner in which you want the Smalltalk object to behave. Keep in mind that the object you are animating is probably just a metaphor of the Smalltalk object you are designing. This mental pen is a transitional entity between the real-world object and the Smalltalk object. (Can you believe that some people can actually animate a Smalltalk object? I wonder what it looks like to them.) Animating your visualization is particularly helpful in modeling the behavior of the object you are designing. If you are having problems animating your object, try anthropomorphism.
What's that?	

JIM	OBJECTIVE WIZARD
	Anthropomorphism is the assignment of human characteristics to a nonhuman creature or an inanimate object.
It sounds like a god complex to me.	
	I am unfamiliar with that terminology.
	In this case, you have an object in mind (literally) and are assigning it a personality—or some lifelike characteristic—in an effort to augment somewhat-lacking visualization efforts. Anthropomorphism is a process humans find especially helpful in relating objects to themselves.
	It is helpful to think in terms of personalities with which you are somewhat familiar.
	Personalities that often work include the following:
	manager mimic dispatcher agent
	Actual people from the problem domain can often be useful as animated objects (in your mind's eye, of course). The benefit derived from using personalities from the problem domain is that it often results in a design that is close to implementation.
How about an example?	
	Sure. Another way of thinking about an object that goes to get information is a messenger or, perhaps, a dog going to fetch a newspaper. The messenger is more capable, but the message interface to the dog is simpler.
	Question: Which of the two "personalities" here best fits your needs: the messenger or the dog?
Hmm, choosing the right metaphor might be important.	

JIM	OBJECTIVE WIZARD
	Indeed, an apt metaphor for a given object in a given situation will lead you to better problem solving.
Do you have any more thinking tools?	
	Yes, many, but only one that I would like to talk about right now.
What is it?	
	Perspective.
Oh?	
	Yes, as an object-oriented thinker you can make several important perspective changes that may help you in your design process. Try these three sometime. Perspective One Observe the object from a point of view outside the object. Perspective Two Observe the object from a point of view inside the object. Perspective Three Become the object and, in effect, observe yourself.
Whew. I'm going to need an example of this.	
	Let us use the tear-out subscription card example and view the visualized card from the three perspectives: Perspective One From outside the object, you tell it where to send the future issues and how you will pay for the lot of them—and then you tell it to do its stuff. Perspective Two From inside the object, you can watch what adding of information does to your instance variables, any internal flags you might set, and what to do if the user sends you

JIM	OBJECTIVE WIZARD
	off without filling in an address (that is, using a default address).
	Perspective Three
	By becoming the object, you access all your information, and then you go out and actually acquire the information. You are put into the mail, and you are delivered to the place where the information is kept.
	Now, do you return with the information or just tell the recipient what to send and where to send it?
	What decisions are you making?
	Are you confused, Jim?
Wiz, I don't think I am in Kansas anymore.	
	Where did you hear about Kansas? We will not discuss Kansas at this juncture.
Never mind.	
	All right.
How can I put this all together?	
	Pick a problem of interest to you.
Now?	
	Yes!
Okay. I'm ready.	
	Sit comfortably. Close your eyes, and think about an object you have specified in your problem scope.
	Ask yourself, "What object do I know about that is similar to this object?" (Metaphor)
	When you find a suitable metaphor, visualize it in your mind's eye. Observe and learn from what you see. (Visualization)
	When you have a visualization, make it behave in some problem domain manner. Learn from your animation's

JIM | OBJECTIVE WIZARD

behaviors. Watch the individual behaviors and the sequence in which they happen. (Animation)

Try assigning your object's responsibilities to a personality type. Run your animation with this personality substituted for your original metaphor. (Anthropomorphism)

Continue to watch your anthropomorphic, animated visualization of a metaphorical object from your problem domain—then change your perspective. Move your mind's eye inside the visualization, perhaps to study a particular variable or characteristic. Become that variable or characteristic and note the changes that are happening to you. (Perspective)

Wow! How can I learn to make this easier?

Practice.

This is not programming as I learned it.

You are right—in fact, this is not programming at all.

It is a particular style of thinking/problem solving/analysis. Experiment with these techniques. They work, and they will make you a better object-oriented thinker and designer. In addition, these techniques fit in well with the basic design methodology that we use here in ObjectLand.

Thinking strategies such as these represent what is generally called "analysis" in other paradigms. However, do not impose other paradigms; do not think of these ObjectLand styles as simply analysis. Instead, as you can see, object-oriented design and development methodologies can be quite unconventional.

Methodologies?

Yes. As in all programming paradigms, there are methodologies to guide the innocent through the processes of analysis, design, and development.

What is the methodology you use?

JIM	OBJECTIVE WIZARD
	I use a fundamental methodology that is simple but effective. I think you will like it. How about starting with that one?
I'm all ears.	
	In this methodology, the completed design is never more than six steps away. The steps are as follows: 1. State the problem. 2. Visualize, and so on. 3. Objectify and classify. 4. Describe object states. 5. Describe the message interfaces. 6. Write the method code. While these steps appear to be sequential, they are often used in a rather gestalt-based iteration, which means that they are used in what you might call an intuitive style that attains the overall goal. In other words, expect to iterate around in the methodology while you are working on the design. I want to discuss these steps one at a time.
Let's go.	
	The first step is to state the problem. Your problem statement can take any form you like, as long as it is an effective way for you to describe the problem. Most people use a text description initially and then condense it into some form of graphical representation having circles, lines, etc. The statement should provide enough information about the problem so that you can begin to design a solution. It must also state what the problem is not. The "problem is not" part of the description will provide a scope for the problem.
Any suggestions on how I can do this?	
	Sure. Use an erasable medium, such as a chalkboard, white board, or computer. Multiple drawing colors are also useful. Sit and think before writing anything down.

JIM	OBJECTIVE WIZARD
What's the next step?	
	The second step is to visualize the problem. If it is a window-based application, draw the window. Drawing in this sense is very much an extension of the statement of the problem, and it is a big step in the iterative process of moving from the problem to the solution. In addition, this step will help to make the problem tangible. help to bring out complexity. create a piece of the solution. provide an early focus on appearance. force a description of interactions. have to be done eventually, anyway.
Any hints?	
	Yes. List any menu options. Pay attention to the relationships between windows and panes.
What is step 3?	
	Identify objects in your visualization, and then group them into classes. This step is the class definition step. You can do this step on paper, but a faster way to do it is in your mind. Think initially about your classes, and then use the System Browser to define them in your Squeak environment. Designing your classes in the System Browser allows you to begin developing concurrently with your initial design process.
I've got the classes. Now what do I do with them?	
	In step 4, you describe the information contained in your classes. The information contained in your objects will be defined in the class and instance variables of the object. The information each object has to maintain can be identified by thinking about the behavior of the object.

JIM	OBJECTIVE WIZARD
	At this point, if you are having some trouble determining what information your object should contain, use some object-oriented thinking tools. For example, change perspective. Pretend to be using the object or pretend to be the object itself.
	You might as well enter your class definitions using the class hierarchy browser now.
Hints?	
	Yes.
	Do not worry about getting it right the first time.
Are we done yet?	
	Not yet. In step 5, you list the message interfaces for each of your classes. Remember: since objects interface with the real world only through their message interfaces, the outcome of this step will determine, in large part, the behavior of your objects. Use the menus from the window drawing in step 2. Each menu option is an action and should be reflected in the message interface.
	When you are dealing with a large number of messages (more than ten), list them in functional groups—or categories—that reflect facets of the object's behavior.
So what is step 6?	
	Write the methods for implementing each message. The steps prior to step 6 have consisted of design with a little code writing (yes, class definition is code writing). Step 6 is code writing in a more conventional sense. When you are done with step 6, you will have completed the first pass on your project. It will behave as you designed it to behave, and it will be ready to show you how it works. The next step in the overall process is to iterate over the steps in the methodology to improve your design.
	Do this until you are satisfied.
I'd like to try this methodology out. How about it?	

JIM	OBJECTIVE WIZARD
	Sure. The To Do List has some ideas for you. But before you go…
	Jim, look deep into my implementation. What do you see now?
My Gawd!	
You're full of objects!	
	Jim, you have made the paradigm shift. Our future conversations should prove very interesting.
	Do svidaniya.

Summary

New Terms

Metaphor

Visualization

Animation

Anthropomorphism

Perspective

Methodology

Iterative Design and Development

What Did You Learn?

- Some differences between conventional analysis and object-oriented thinking.
- Some general thinking "tools"—metaphor, visualization, animation, anthropomorphism, and perspective—that can be useful in object-oriented thinking.
- A simple six-step, object-oriented design and development methodology.

Words of Wisdom

Define your problem.

Problem definition may not be half the battle, but it does keep you from wasting your time solving a problem that doesn't need to be solved.

Defining what your problem *isn't* is at least as important as defining what your problem *is*.

When you first start designing a solution to a problem, keep things as changeable as possible. The more you design, the more you will understand the problem, which will modify your design some more. This loop is more productive if it is easy to change the design.

Remember that the easiest place to make changes is in your head: writing things down makes them significantly harder to change.

To Do List

One of the nice things about the design and development methodology presented in this chapter is that a first-pass design can be done very quickly. Do a design of three of the following in no more than a half hour each. Fifteen minutes is better.

1. Design an appointment book.
2. Design a control system for an automated donut factory.

3. Design an inventory system for a collector (stamp, coin, car, whatever).
4. Design an investment tracking system.

When you are finished, evaluate your performance by asking yourself the following questions:

How much time did I take for each design?
Did I get faster on the latter designs?
What recording media did I use (paper, white board, computer, etc.)?
Did I get through all five steps for each problem?

Design your current project—or a part of it that's small enough to move through steps 1 through 5 in one hour. If it takes less than an hour, good.

Take one of the first-pass design problems from the list above and refine the design. Don't spend more than an hour. Try to get to the point where you are actually writing code for some of the messages in your object's message interface.

Try experimenting with different ways of doing your designs. One change you can make is to do as much of the design as you can in your head before writing things down. We have found that the more you can do in this fashion, the faster the problem is solved. With practice, you may find that the first four or five design iterations can happen without writing down more than a few notes.

When you write down your design, use an easily changeable medium. In ObjectLand, we prefer a large white board with several colored markers. If possible, try doing a tandem design with a co-worker. This approach takes longer, but the designs are more robust.

14

An Introduction to Morphic

Contents at: 'Chapter 14'

#(

GUIs

MVC
  model
  view
  controller

morphs

Object Explorer

new morph... menu
  widgets
  windows

Morphic design
  concreteness
  liveness

`Morph`
  `World`

`PasteUpMorph`
  linear layout

`AlignmentMorph`

`HandMorph`

Morphic Event).

Questions of Interest

- What is a GUI?
- What is MVC?
- Why Morphic?
- What are the responsibilities of some Morphic classes?

Introduction

In this chapter, you will be introduced to the concept of a graphical user interface, something that you have been using all along as you employ Squeak. You will get a little information on MVC, an older graphical user interface, and then be introduced to Morphic, the interface we've been using in this book.

Then you will receive some information on submorphs and on the responsibilities of just a few Morphic classes. This information on Morphic classes will be very important for proceeding to the final chapter, where you will put your understanding of Morphic classes more fully into practice.

Goals for This Chapter

- To understand what a GUI is and that you have been using one.
- To become briefly familiar with MVC as a GUI.
- To become more familiar with the Morphic GUI.
- To get a taste of the Object Explorer tool.
- To understand the concept of submorphs.
- To understand the responsibilities of five specific `Morph` classes.

JIM	OBJECTIVE WIZARD
Okay, here I am—ready as I'll ever be.	
	Glad to hear it. Let us get started with your introduction to Morphic. One of the features that users have come to identify closely with personal computers is the graphical user interface, often simply referred to as a GUI.
Gooey. Rhymes with chewy. Any chance we can discuss this over a pizza?	
	No, Jim. You can have a snack later. For now, let us talk about GUIs. The construction of GUIs was one of the first areas in software development in which object orientation really got to demonstrate its power and flexibility. I have heard GUIs referred to as the first OO Killer App.
That's a good way for me to remember them: killer apps.	
	Focus, Jim, shall we? You are about to begin an investigation into the GUIs that are present in the Squeak environment. Careful analysis of the preceding sentence will reveal the usage of the plural of GUI. This usage is employed because the Squeak environment can make use of two separate user interface frameworks: MVC and Morphic.
Let's start with Morphic. That's at least something I've heard before.	
	Indeed, it is. Thus far, all of your learning in ObjectLand has been carried out using the Morphic GUI framework. In your first trip to the ObjectLand library, you were introduced to projects, menus, the Workspace, and the Transcript.
And I was introduced to the Objective Librarian.	
	Yes, you met the Objective Librarian. Very good librarian.
I'll say! She's very good.	

JIM	OBJECTIVE WIZARD
	Anyway, on that trip to the library, you were introduced to tools such as the Transcript. Each of these tools was, at its heart, an artifact of the Morphic GUI framework. On your second trip to the library, you were introduced to many of the software development tools that are available in the Squeak environment. These tools are also built from the Mophic framework.
Yes, I remember.	
	Well, the Objective Librarian did not give you the whole story. As you will soon see, even though we often made you aware that you were using a part of the Morphic framework, other parts of the Morphic framework have sometimes been active behind the scenes without your knowledge.
Really? So, I don't really understand as much about Morphic as I thought.	
	That is why you have found yourself here, once again asking of my valuable time and vast knowledge. The aim of this section of your instruction is to further your understanding of the underpinnings of the Morphic framework. While you are here, you are going to investigate several Morphic classes: `Morph`, `PasteUpMorph`, `AlignmentMorph`, `HandMorph`, and `MorphicEvents`. As mentioned earlier, in addition to Morphic, the Squeak environment supports a second GUI framework, known as MVC.
What's the difference?	
	MVC is the older of the two interface frameworks that Squeak supports. In fact, MVC is perhaps the oldest paradigm for building a GUI.
I know I've heard this before, but can you remind me anyway? What does MVC stand for?	
	The letters in the acronym MVC stand for the components of the following triad: Model, View, and Controller.

JIM	OBJECTIVE WIZARD
Okay, go on.	
	Certainly, character-based terminals were a type of graphical user interface, but they aren't what personal computer users currently associate with the idea of a GUI. To make a long story short, the primary aim of MVC is what software developers often refer to as the separation of concerns. You can get a sense for how MVC attempts to achieve this goal by looking at each of the pieces of the triad in turn. Let us start with the *model*. Quite simply, the responsibility of the model is to encapsulate the application domain's state and behavior. The complexity of the Smalltalk code necessary to represent the application domain is determined by the complexity of the application domain. In very simple situations, the model may map to a class that is already defined in the Smalltalk class library: an `Integer`, a `String`, an `OrderedCollection`. In more involved applications, it may be necessary to create one or more user-defined classes to satisfy the requirements of the domain.
I think I understand. And the view?	
	The *view* is the graphical representation of the model that is currently being displayed by your application. A model can have many views, but each view has only one model. At the request of the user, the view that is being displayed may be changed.
Hmm. Okay, the model maps the application domain's state and behavior, and the view represents the model graphically. Right?	
	Yes. Last, but not least, the *controller* is responsible for managing the user's inputs. The controller sends messages to the model, and it acts as a go-between for the model and the view. Controllers are often thought of as being paired with a specific view. This pair, in turn, is attached to a particular model.

Jim	Objective Wizard
MVC. Model. View. Controller.	
Go on. I'll try to keep up.	
	The user interface of an application is one of the areas that are most likely to change during an application's lifetime. Ultimately, the MVC paradigm facilitates making changes in an application in a manner that minimizes the impact on the rest of the system.
	Often, the view and the controller are coupled so tightly that recent variations of MVC have combined the two into one. One instance of this tendency can be seen in the Microsoft Foundation Classes' Document-View architecture.
I've never heard of that architecture. But you said something about the user interface. Do I need to know more about that, since I'm a user?	
	Prior to Squeak release 3.0, MVC was the default Squeak interface. However, as of 3.0, this role has been taken over by Morphic. This changeover lets users know, in no uncertain terms, that the future interface for Squeak is the Morphic framework. So, with that in mind, you should prepare to learn as much as you can about Morphic.
Should I still keep MVC in mind? Or can I forget about it and just worry about Morphic?	
	As mentioned earlier, a goal of MVC is to separate UI classes from the domain model of your application. This is still a valid goal in Morphic. In fact, even today MVC coexists in Squeak with Morphic in a hybrid form. If you investigate Squeak's development tools, you can still see vestigial traces of MVC. This situation, however, is beyond the scope of this book.
Yes, obviously it's too complex for me right now. I'll just worry about Morphic.	

JIM	OBJECTIVE WIZARD
	Fine. But you should keep in mind that MVC exists.
Back to these GUIs. What do I need to know?	
	The goal of a graphical user interface is to facilitate interaction between a human user—such as yourself—and the computer. In order to begin to understand how Morphic accomplishes this goal, let us see what Squeak has to say about Morphic. You are going use the System Browser to check for the class comment about `Morph`. Go ahead and open a System Browser if you have not done so. The `Morph` class is located in the `Morphic-Kernel` category. After selecting Morph, red-button click the `?` that is located between the tiny panes labeled `instance` and `class`.
Let's not rush here. Go slowly.	
	Have you completed this action?
Yes. Is this the class comment I see?	

	Yes, this action will display the class comment in the lower pane of the browser. For the time being, you need to be concerned with the following parts of the comment:
	`A morph (from the Greek "shape" or "form") is an interactive graphical object.`
	`All morphs owned by a morph are held in submorphs.`
	`All coordinates are global screen coordinates.`
	Let us evaluate each section of this comment in turn.

Okay. The first part of the comment says that a morph is a graphical object.	
	The first part of the comment is quite straightforward and satisfies what your intuition should already be telling you about morphs. A `Morph`, or any of its subclasses, is a visual

JIM	OBJECTIVE WIZARD
	representation that can be manipulated (picked up, moved about, dismissed, and so on).
	The second part of the comment is concerned with the submorph relationship. We will go into more detail about this relationship a bit later, but for now you should be aware that a `Morph` can have ownership over other morphs. These owned morphs are referred to as submorphs.
That makes sense, I guess.	
	The third part of the comment has to do with how the position of a `Morph` is represented with respect to the displayed Squeak environment. Before you examine this aspect of morphs, you should know a bit more about how the environment of the Squeak display is organized.
If you think that's what I should know, then I'm sure that's what you'll tell me next.	
	Jim, would you like to take a little break for some coffee? I sense you weakening.
Yes, that'd be great. Just give me a few minutes. This is a lot to keep track of, and I can see that there's important stuff ahead.	
	Ready now? Shall we get started again?
Let's. I'm ready. Now, you were saying something about how the environment of the Squeak display is organized.	
	Very good. Like most 2-D graphical environments, Squeak makes use of the Cartesian coordinate system. In this system, a location on the surface is represented by `x`- and y-values. As with everything in ObjectLand, the `x`- and y-values are objects. In this instance, they are `Integer` objects. They, in turn, are encapsulated within a `Point` object. In the Squeak environment, the upper left corner of the display is at `x = 0`

JIM	OBJECTIVE WIZARD
	and y = 0. If your Squeak environment is currently displaying in full screen mode, the value of the lower right corner of the display will be equivalent to the resolution of your monitor.
	You should take some time now to investigate how a morph inhabits the Squeak coordinate system. You can carry out this investigation quite effectively by taking a moment to become familiar with another Squeak tool—the Object Explorer.
	The Object Explorer, or just Explorer, is probably the most appropriately named tool that you will ever encounter.
Terrific. Explorer sounds incredibly useful.	
	It certainly can be. The Explorer uses a tree-based model of an object to allow the contents of an object to be inspected. Specifically, clicking on the items that are shown in an Explorer will display the current state of the selected item. You can even open another Explorer on the selected item.
How do I use this tool?	
	One way of starting a new Explorer is from a menu. First, you will want to go ahead and create a new `RectangleMorph`. Enter the following Smalltalk expression in a Workspace:
	`RectangleMorph new openInWorld.`
	Now, evaluate the expression via a `do it` or a `print it`.
I get a new rectangle, then.	
	Yes, a new `RectangleMorph` will be created and placed in the upper right corner of the Squeak environment. Blue-button click your newly created morph in order to activate its halo.
Okay, I have the halo activated.	
	Select the red menu handle. From the resulting Rectangle menu, select the **debug...** menu item. This will result in a submenu being displayed. Choose the **explore morph** menu item. This opens a new Explorer.

JIM	OBJECTIVE WIZARD
Yes, I see. Now where should I click?	
	Click on the small triangle in order to display the contents of the object in question. You can now verify the fact that morphs are displayed using the global screen coordinates.
Now, the Objective Librarian said that there's another way to create new morphs.	
	In the example above, you created a new `RectangleMorph` from within a Workspace. As mentioned in your second trip to the library, there is another way that you can instantiate new morphs. If you have not taken the time yet, you can—and should—experiment with the wide variety of morphs that are available to you from the **new morph...** menu item of the World menu. Much earlier, it was suggested that you take a look at the demo and games morphs. By now, you have probably whiled away many hours playing Tetris.
Well, I must admit I've spent my fair share of time with Tetris. Those moving eye morphs, by the way, are starting to creep me out a little.	
	You should probably expand your horizons a bit and take a look at the morphs that are available from the **Widgets** and **Windows** menu items.
Good idea. Hey, where did Morphic come from, anyway?	
	Good question, Jim. Morphic was originally developed as an interface framework for a research programming language named Self. One of the original goals of the design of Morphic was to allow users to get closer to objects. This goal was achieved by making morphs more concrete than the graphical objects in other frameworks.

Jim	Objective Wizard
How did they make morphs more concrete than objects were in other frameworks? I don't understand how I'm closer to objects.	
	Part of this goal was achieved by taking advantage of the human nervous system. That is probably why you do not even notice the concreteness that Morphic employs. You might remember that the Objective Librarian pointed out that morphs have a shadow painted on the screen when they have been grabbed. This shadow gives the appearance that the morph has actually been lifted off of the screen. This effect makes the morph seem tangible.
I think I understand. The shadow replicates my sense of reality. When I grab a morph, a shadow appears to make me—unconsciously—aware that I've lifted it. That's pretty subtle.	
	Indeed, it is. Another facet of morphs that affords more direct access is the halo. The halo, which was also described by the Objective Librarian, gives the user the ability to directly manipulate the most important aspects of the morph.
The halo is more obvious. It's one of the things I like best about morphs. It makes me feel as if the aspects are right there at my disposal.	
	The halo has a lot of benefits, as I'm sure you are discovering. Another design goal for the Morphic interface was a quality that its creators referred to as *liveness*. One way in which the Morphic framework attempts to satisfy this goal is through its ability to support and incorporate animation.

JIM | OBJECTIVE WIZARD

Jim: So *liveness* is action and liveliness. It's the fun part of Morphic, then?

Objective Wizard: Sort of. Morphic is definitely designed for clarity but also to keep you actively engaged. The Morphic framework is also designed so that morphs can update themselves. This aspect is an improvement over interfaces in which the user must consciously interact with a graphical object in order to see changes in the object's status.

Jim: Yeah, it's more of a give-and-take interaction instead of me always bullying things.

How does the idea of morphs owning other morphs fit into these design goals?

Objective Wizard: As mentioned above, in the Morphic framework, one morph can own another. An outcome of this relationship is that morphs can be composed. A morph that has submorphs is said to be a composite morph.

This containment relationship can be described by the tree data structure. In the context of Morphic, this means that there is a root morph that can have any number of submorphs (think children, think big branches). These submorphs can, in turn, have their own submorphs (grandchildren or small branches). However, a morph can have only one owner. In keeping with the tree metaphor, we also have leaves to consider. A leaf is the terminal part of the tree. In Morphic, this is a submorph that has no submorphs of its own.

Jim: The spinster aunts and dandy uncles? I like these metaphors.

Now, what about morph classes?

Objective Wizard: There are several key classes in the Morphic framework, and an investigation of them will reveal much about the nature and organization of the Morphic user interface. The Mor-

JIM | OBJECTIVE WIZARD

phic classes that you are going to be exposed to in the next few sections are as follows:

```
Morph
PasteUpMorph
AlignmentMorph
HandMorph
MorphicEvent
```

Of the classes presented in the list above, `PasteUpMorph`, `AlignmentMorph`, and `HandMorph` are ultimately children of `Morph`. However, there are some classes in the Morphic framework that are not subclasses of `Morph`. Among those classes that we will be discussing, the `MorphicEvent` class is an example of a class that is not a part of the `Morph` hierarchy.

Is that the only class that's not part of this hierarchy? Or is it just the only one in these examples?

There are other helper classes that are not subclasses of `Morph` or any of its descendants. While we will not be discussing these classes, if you are interested, you can take a look at the classes in the `Morphic-Kernel` category. Specifically, you should investigate the class `MorphExtension`.

The `Morph` class is the root, or base class, of those classes in the Morphic framework that can be drawn on the display.

I guess I need to know more about the `Morph` class. Can you tell me about that?

`Morph` is an enormously complicated class. This complexity is reflected in the fact that in the current Squeak image, there are a total of 942 methods in 50 categories in the `Morph` class.

Oh my! Do I need to know something about all those methods? Why are there so many?

JIM	OBJECTIVE WIZARD
	Do not worry, Jim. I will not be bombarding you with what you can do with 942 methods, but you do need to keep in mind the extent of this class. Further inspection of the categories reveals a wide range of responsibilities that have fallen upon the `Morph` class. Many of the categories, such as `drawing`, `dropping/grabbing`, `event handling`, `geometry`, `submorphs-accessing`, `submorphs-add/remove`, and `visual properties`, seem immediately consistent with the idea of a graphical object that can be manipulated on the screen. Others, such as `parts-bin` and `piano rolls`, do not. In sum, the Morph class is probably too large an entity for you to study in isolation. A good approach would be to study some of its simpler subclasses and to try and get a sense of Morph via those relationships. In fact, this is exactly the approach that we will take in the following chapter.
That seems reasonable. Shall we begin with `PasteUpMorph`?	
	There is an old joke about a question on a Philosophy 101 final exam. The question reads simply, "Define the universe. Give three examples." Here in ObjectLand, we do not have a better answer for that question than anyone else. That said, we certainly know how to define our `World`. In Smalltalk terms, the `World` is a global variable whose value is an instantiated `PasteUpMorph`. In terms of the Morphic framework, the `World` is the owner of all of the morphs that you see drawn on your display. On a related note, in previous versions of Squeak, the `PasteUpMorph` was known as `WorldMorph`. The next class from our list, the `AlignmentMorph` class, is responsible for positioning and fitting its submorphs to the constraints of the available space. The default behavior of an `AlignmentMorph` is to lay out its submorphs linearly.
Okay. Two classes down, two to go?	

JIM	OBJECTIVE WIZARD
	First, let me add something about linear layout. The linear layout methodology works as follows. The first submorph is placed at the leftmost edge of the available bounds, the next submorph is placed on the first submorph's rightmost edge, and so on.
Just back and forth—okay.	
Go on.	
	The `HandMorph` class is the Morphic realization of the cursor.
I get it. Hand, cursor.	
	The cursor that you maneuver around your display is actually an instance of the `HandMorph` class. Even though the cursor moves around on the surface of the World, it is not part of it.
I didn't want to say anything, but I must admit that I wasn't sure I was getting these classes. I understand this one, though, because I understand how the cursor must be an instance of the idea of *hand*. It seems pretty simple.	
	Now, if the only responsibility of the `HandMorph` class was to point at things, it would not be a particularly interesting class. Quite to the contrary, the `HandMorph` class has a great deal of responsibility and thus is not exactly simple. Think about what happens when you pick up a morph and move it to a new location. This action is accomplished by making the selected object a submorph of the cursor for the duration of the move.
Oh, I hadn't really thought about it that way.	
	Earlier, I mentioned that the cursor is not part of the World. By extension, this fact is also true for any submorph that belongs to the cursor. As a result, when you grab a morph and move it to another location, it is removed from the

Jim	Objective Wizard
	World for the duration of the move. At the conclusion of the move, it is added back to the World.
Hmm, that's a little more complicated. Sometimes there's a lot more going on than I think there is.	
	I suppose that is the human condition in a nutshell, Jim. In this case, there is more yet. The `HandMorph` class, in its instantiated role as a cursor, is also the event source for much of a user's input. The `HandMorph` is also responsible for determining the receiver of the events that it generates.
Wow, the class that I would've guessed was the most straightforward seems to be the most complicated. Now I'm not sure if I get it.	
	I think you are getting it, Jim. You are on the right track when you say that `HandMorph` is straightforward. When you think about it, all the responsibilities of the class make sense. You just need to remember how much is going on at once when you perform any task. These classes are very straightforward, but a class can be complex.
I think I understand what you're saying. I just need to think things through and not jump to conclusions at first glance. Now, there was one more class on our list, right?	
	Yes. Remember how we discussed controllers when we were talking about MVC?
Sort of, but you said I didn't have to remember anything about MVC.	

JIM	OBJECTIVE WIZARD
	That is true, but I wanted you to remember that it existed and that *C* stands for *controller*. Well, in a sense, all of the responsibilities of the controller are already part of the Morphic framework. The input actions of the user—pressing a key on the keyboard, moving the mouse, clicking (both down and up) with the mouse, and combinations of these activities—are described by the `MorphicEvent` class. As mentioned earlier, the `Morph` class has a method category called `event handling`. Many of these methods take an instance of the `MorphicEvent` class as an argument.
Wow, this class sounds complex too, especially when you say "combinations." How much do I need to know about these four classes, anyway?	
	Jim, I think we are finished for now. Just remember the basics we covered here, and you can put these concepts into practice when we meet again.
This stuff's really important. Let me run through some of it quickly while you're around. So, the `Morph` class is the parent class of `PasteUpMorph`, `AlignmentMorph`, and `HandMorph`. It's responsible for the interactive, graphical behaviors that are common to all morphs.	
	Yes, that is correct.
And when I think of a `PasteUpMorph`, I should think of everything that is part of the Squeak environment that I am currently viewing. The whole `World` in other words.	
	Right again, Jim.

JIM	OBJECTIVE WIZARD
Instances of the `AlignmentMorph` class are responsible for "lining up" all of the submorphs that they own.	
	Yes.
The most important `HandMorph` is the cursor?	
	You are on a roll, Jim.
Last but not least, instances of the `MorphicEvent` class are responsible for handling all of my input and keeping everything moving along.	
	Five for five Jim. Outstanding.
Is that all for now?	
	That is all—good-bye.

Summary

New Terms

GUI (Graphical User Interface)	MVC (Model, View, Controller)
Object Explorer	Submorphs
Concreteness	Liveness

What Did You Learn?

- What a GUI is and that you have been using one when you've used Squeak.
- MVC is the old interface that has been superseded by Morphic.
- The basics of Morphic as a GUI, including the fact that it exhibits concreteness and liveness.
- The basics of the Object Explorer as a tool for, of course, exploring.
- The basics of the morph-submorph relationship.
- The responsibilities of five Morphic classes:

```
Morph
PasteUpMorph
AlignmentMorph
HandMorph
MorphicEvent
```

Words of Wisdom

The concept of morph ownership is based on the tree data structure.

Morphic, as a GUI, feels tangible (concrete) and active (live), which makes the environment and your interaction with it feel more natural to you. A task sometimes feels simpler than it really is—so, think about what's going on behind the scenes as you complete tasks.

The Morphic classes are straightforward, but they are not simple. A class can be complex when it is responsible for numerous tasks, some of which might not be immediately evident to you.

To Do List

In order to experiment even more with some morphs, try out this list of common Morphic getter messages.

```
owner
submorphs
```

```
submorphCount
bounds
boundsInWorld
isInWorld
world
```

Using the Object Explorer, see if you can identify all of the morphs in a project—flaps, Alignment, Navigator, and so on.

Find another way to open an Explorer on an object. (*Hint:* Think workspace.)

15

Morphic Programming

Contents at: 'Chapter 15'

#(

changing color
  Morphic menu handle
  color palette
  eyedropper cursor

embedding

`BorderedMorph`

`MovingEyeMorph`

Inspector
  Debug... menu item

`RectangleMorph`

`GreenRectangleMorph`

`SimpleButtonMorph`
  `HandlesMouseDown:evt`

`IconicButtonMorph`
  Disassembling a composite morph

using inheritance
  create `SmileyIconicButton`

Forms

`AnimatedSmileyIconicButton`
  event handling
  animation).

Questions of Interest

- How can I change a morph's color?
- How can I embed one morph in another?
- How can I use inheritance to create a Morphic class?
- Are there different ways of moving morphs?
- How can I create a simple animation?

Introduction

This chapter builds directly on the preceding chapter and puts into practice some of the important concepts from that chapter. This chapter is very hands-on—be prepared to *do* a lot as you move through the discussion here.

You will gain some experience manipulating morphs. On a simple level, you will learn how to change a morph's color. On a more complex level, you will learn how to construct a simple animation sequence. In the process, you will be introduced to several new morphs and some of their potential.

Goals for This Chapter

- To change the color of a morph.
- To understand some of the capabilities of an Inspector.
- To understand more fully the concepts of embedding and disassembling morphs.
- To create a new class of morphs.
- To be introduced to a morph that must be moved by a handle.
- To use your knowledge of morphs to create a short, simple animation.

JIM	OBJECTIVE WIZARD

Jim: That last chapter was a doozy. I'm not sure I've kept track of everything.

Objective Wizard: That is fine, Jim, because our impending discussion will allow you to accomplish something useful and concrete to reinforce the more general discussion that we had when we were last together. In order to begin, let us walk down the specific inheritance hierarchy that starts at `Morph` and ends at `IconicButtonMorph`. The classes that belong to this portion of the Morphic hierarchy are shown below.

```
Morph
 BorderedMorph
  RectangleMorph
   SimpleButtonMorph
    IconicButtonMorph
```

You are going to learn how to interact with these classes in a programmatic manner.

Jim: That sounds important. How will I do that?

Objective Wizard: Sometimes you will be making use of the Morphic menu options. Other times, you will be using a Workspace to create instances and to send messages to the instantiated objects. Finally, in two cases, you will be extending the Morphic framework by defining new classes. In the first case, you will extend `RectangleMorph` by creating `GreenRectangleMorph`. In the second case, when you reach the end of this hierarchy, you will extend it—through inheritance—a bit further by first adding `SmileyIconicButton` and then adding `Animated SmileyIconicButton`.

Jim: Okay, we are getting right down to business—but I think I need some more practice with the `Morph` class.

Objective Wizard: I had surmised as much. What is it that humans say—one step forward, two steps back?

Jim | **Objective Wizard**

Objective Wizard: To get a better appreciation for the Morph class, you are going to change the state of an object that was instantiated from the Morph class.

Jim: Do I need to create a new instance of a Morph?

Objective Wizard: Yes. To begin, you will want to create a new instance of a Morph. You can do this by entering the following Smalltalk expression in a Workspace window.

```
Morph new openInWorld.
```

The result that is displayed in the upper left corner of the Squeak environment (at position 0,0) should look like the graphic displayed in Figure 15–1.

Jim: Okay, I've got that! What should I do with it?

Objective Wizard: Our ultimate aim in this case is to change the color of the Morph object. If you have not done so recently, use a system Browser to look at the instance variables of class Morph. You should see the variable color listed among the instance variables.

Jim: Ah, yes. Now what?

Objective Wizard: You are going to effect the change in color via the built-in Morphic menu. You will need to yellow-button click the morph in order to activate its halo. The result will look like Figure 15–2.

Figure 15–1
A Morph

Figure 15–2
A Morph and its halo

JIM	OBJECTIVE WIZARD
Okay, now which icon do I need?	
	The morph's menu is available from the red handle. You should note that the icon in the red handle is meant to suggest that it provides access to the menu. The icons—as simple, visual metaphors—are rather helpful to humans. Go ahead and red-button select the handle.
Okay. Now I have the menu.	
	Does it look like the one in Figure 15–3?
Yep, it does.	
	Great. As shown in the image in Figure 15–3, the menu item that we are interested in is the **fill style**. Selecting this item will result in the display of a submenu.

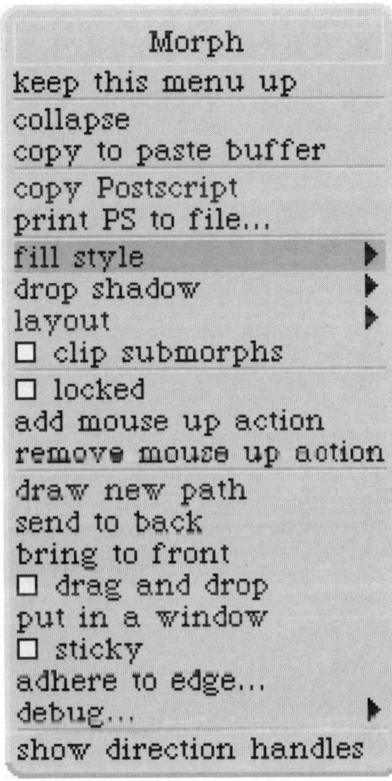

Figure 15–3
The Morph menu

Jim

Yes, the submenu appears. I see a **change color...** item.

Objective Wizard

Good. Select the **change color...** item of the submenu, just as I am showing you in Figure 15–4.

This selection results in the display of two new items: a color palette and an eyedropper cursor.

Jim

Wow, this is getting neat. How do I choose a new color?

Objective Wizard

The cursor is used to select the new color. In the upper right corner of the color palette are two tiny squares. The leftmost square displays the morph's current color. The rightmost square displays the color that the eyedropper cursor is currently over in the color palette. This selected color, as shown in Figure 15–5, is the color that will be chosen when you click the mouse.

Jim

So, I can move the eyedropper over different colors?

Objective Wizard

Exactly. The resulting morph—if one clicks the mouse on this color—is shown in Figure 15–6. I am not partial to blue, although I know it is the favorite color of humans.

change color...
solid fill
gradient fill
bitmap fill
default fill

Figure 15–4 The change color... submenu

Figure 15–5 Color palette

Figure 15–6 A Morph after the color change

JIM	OBJECTIVE WIZARD
I think I'll go for a deep blue.	
What else can I do with a morph like this?	
	In order to investigate the `BorderedMorph`, you are going to be introduced to another Smalltalk development tool—the Inspector—and another Morphic framework concept—embedding. You are going to use the Inspector to observe the effects of embedding one morph inside another.
Embedding sounds complicated.	
	Actually, without being told the name, you were introduced to the concept of embedding in Chapter 14. Basically, *embedding* is the process that Morphic uses to make one morph a submorph of another. You will see how to do this via the same Morphic menu that we used in the preceding section.
So, embedding isn't a new idea for me? Okay, then, let's run for the border.	
	First, you are going to use the **new morph...** menu to create a new `BorderedMorph`. Select the **new morph...** menu item. On the resulting menu, click the very first choice—**keep this menu up**. This choice will display the menu until you choose to dismiss it.
Why keep the menu up?	
	Keeping the menu around will prove to be handy for this section. Just wait. Have you a menu that looks like the one in Figure 15–7?
Yep. Am I to gather that I should select **Kernel**?	
	Very observant, Jim. Choosing the **Kernel** menu item will open a submenu that contains two items. Select `BorderedMorph`, as shown in Figure 15–8.
We must be getting somewhere.	

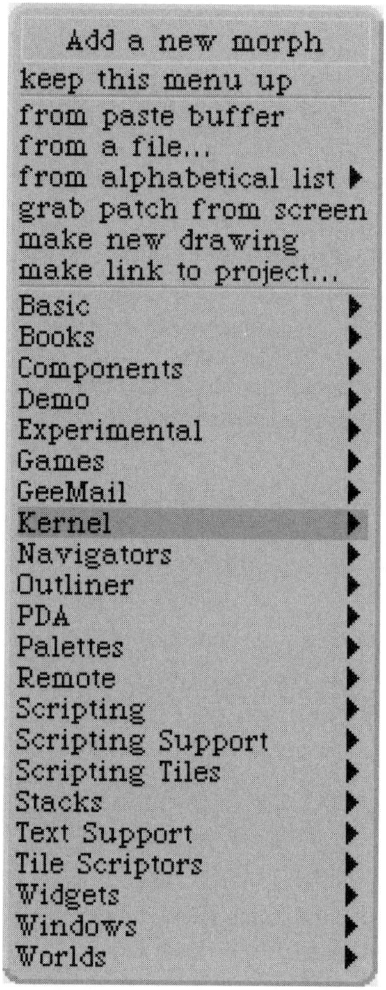

Add a new morph
keep this menu up
from paste buffer
from a file...
from alphabetical list ▶
grab patch from screen
make new drawing
make link to project...
Basic ▶
Books ▶
Components ▶
Demo ▶
Experimental ▶
Games ▶
GeeMail ▶
Kernel ▶
Navigators ▶
Outliner ▶
PDA ▶
Palettes ▶
Remote ▶
Scripting ▶
Scripting Support ▶
Scripting Tiles ▶
Stacks ▶
Text Support ▶
Tile Scriptors ▶
Widgets ▶
Windows ▶
Worlds ▶

Figure 15–7 Add a new morph menu

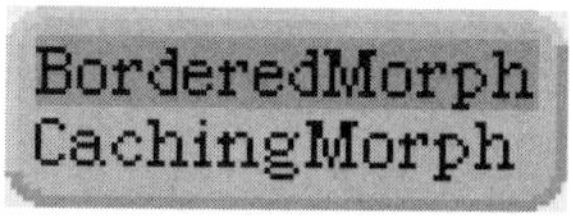

BorderedMorph
CachingMorph

Figure 15–8 BorderedMorph submenu

Yes, this action will result in a new `BorderedMorph` object. The object will be displayed so that it appears as if your cursor is holding it away from the surface of the environment.

Can I put it down?

A mouse click will release the morph and will place it in a location on the `World`.

Okay, now what?

JIM	OBJECTIVE WIZARD
	You are going to embed a `MovingEyeMorph` in the `BorderedMorph` that you just instantiated.
Ah, the roving eye. Sounds great.	
	So, your next action is to create a `MovingEyeMorph`.
How do I do that?	
	The `MovingEyeMorph` can be created using the submenu that is displayed if you choose the **Demo** menu item from the **Add a new morph** menu. A `MovingEyeMorph` is shown in Figure 15–9. Now, you are going to make use of the Inspector.
We're really moving now. What's the Inspector?	
	The *Inspector* is a tool for "inspecting" all of the instance variables of an instantiated object. It is very similar to the Object Explorer that you met in Chapter 14.
How similar? Can I just use the Explorer?	
	The Inspector and the Object Explorer are not the same, Jim. The primary difference between the two is in the way that they present their information. Inspectors also have the useful feature of presenting updated information without being prodded. This feature is an example of the liveness quality of Morphic.
Oh, yes, I remember liveness—a great quality. I can see how updated information is a good thing for me. How do I use the Inspector?	

Figure 15–9 MovingEyeMorph

JIM | **OBJECTIVE WIZARD**

Objective Wizard: In order to use an Inspector, you must first open one. In this case, you want to inspect the `BorderedMorph` object.

Jim: Should I open an Inspector on my roving eye?

Objective Wizard: You can also open an Inspector on the `MovingEyeMorph`, but it is not absolutely necessary.

Jim: Okay, let's skip it then.

Objective Wizard: I assumed you would take that stance.

On the Morph menu that is available from the red halo handle, you should select the **debug...** menu item. As shown in Figure 15–10, choose the **inspect morph** option from the submenu.

The Inspector should look very similar—but not identical—to the one shown in Figure 15–11.

Jim: Why won't it look the same? That always concerns me.

keep this menu up
inspect morph
inspect owner chain
explore morph
browse morph class
make own subclass
internal name
save morph in file
call #tempCommand
define #tempCommand
control-menu...
edit balloon help

Figure 15–10 A Morphic submenu

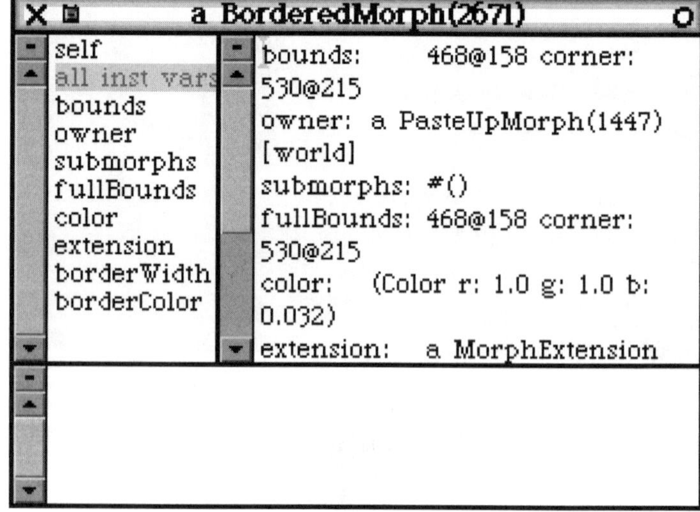

Figure 15–11 BorderedMorph inspector

JIM	OBJECTIVE WIZARD
	Remember, your Inspector will display values that are specific to your system. You should take note of the fact that the `BorderedMorph` does not, at present, have any submorphs.
Okay, mine looks like the one in Figure 15–11.	
	Good. Next, pick up the `MovingEyeMorph` and place it on top of the `BorderedMorph`. The color of the `BorderedMorph` was changed to yellow, so that it would be easier for you to see the images. The image in Figure 15–12 shows the `MovingEyeMorph` suspended over the `BorderedMorph`.
Okay. I see that it's suspended because of the shadow. That's concreteness.	
	Yes, now continue your observations, Jim. By using the Inspector, you can observe that the `MovingEyeMorph` is still not a submorph of the `BorderedMorph`. Next, you need to bring up the Morphic menu for the `MovingEyeMorph`, which is shown in Figure 15–13. You should select the **embed...** option from the menu. This selection will result in display of the submenu shown in Figure 15–14.
And, as in your example, I should choose the **BorderedMorph** item?	
	Yes, by choosing **BorderedMorph**, you will embed the `MovingEyeMorph` in the `BorderedMorph`. The result of this action is shown in the updated Inspector in Figure 15–15.

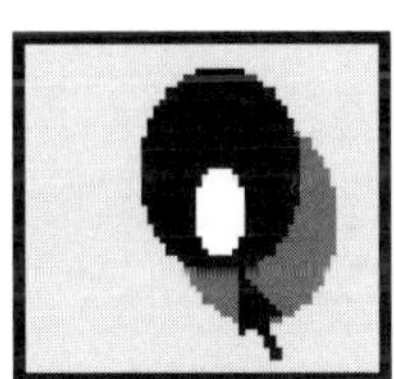

Figure 15–12 A MovingEyeMorph over a BorderedMorph

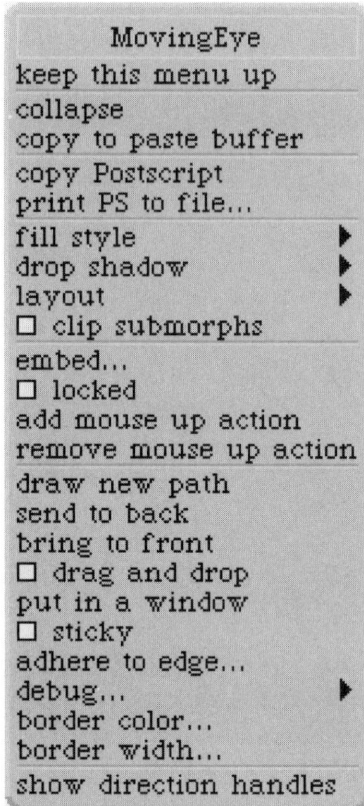

Figure 15–13 MovingEyeMorph menu

Figure 15–14 Submenu to embed a MovingEyeMorph in a BorderedMorph

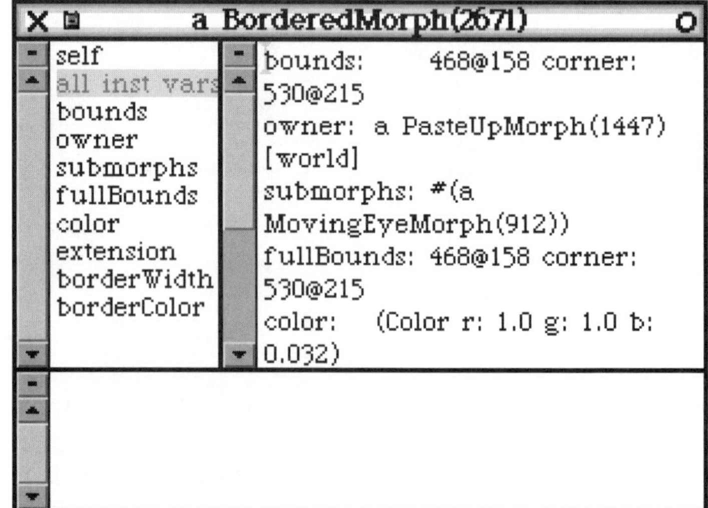

Figure 15–15 Updated BorderedMorph inspector

The inspector now shows that the `BorderedMorph` does indeed have a submorph—a `MovingEyeMorph`.

Wow! So, I've made a bordered morph, and I've made something a submorph.

What's next?

Now you are going to extend the `RectangleMorph` class and create your own class. The only difference between the standard `RectangleMorph` and your class will be the default color.

Okay.

JIM

OBJECTIVE WIZARD

As shown in Figure 15–16, the current default color for instances of the RectangleMorph class is gray.

The defaultColor method provides this behavior for the RectangleMorph class. The defaultColor method has been assigned to the visual properties category. When you create your new class, this method is the one that you will override.

Okay, let's make the default color blue.

Given that I have a fondness for green, I will make green the default color for the new class. Many human beings can't tell the difference between many shades of green and blue, but they are distinct. This color will also provide us with a name for the new class: GreenRectangleMorph.

As you have seen before, the tool for extending the system is the System Browser. Assuming that you already have a System Browser open, go ahead and create a new class in the ObjectLand category. As mentioned above, the name of the new class is GreenRectangleMorph. The new class should be a subclass of RectangleMorph. The Smalltalk code that you have entered in the template in the lower pane should be the following:

```
RectangleMorph subclass:
#GreenRectangleMorph
   instanceVariableNames: ''
   classVariableNames: ''
   poolDictionaries: ''
   category: 'ObjectLand'
```

The next thing that you will want to do is to add a new method category.

Figure 15–16
A RectangleMorph

JIM	OBJECTIVE WIZARD
This stuff is moving pretty fast for me now. Take it one step at a time here. Okay, how do I add a new method category?	
	A yellow-button click over the third pane in the System Browser will bring up a menu that allows you to add a new category. Selecting the **new category...** menu item will result in display of the menu shown in Figure 15–17. As mentioned earlier, the method that you want to override is a member of the `visual properties` category. That category is highlighted in the image in Figure 15–17. Once you have specified the category, then it is time to add the method itself. Select the newly added category in the third pane.
Okay. I think I've got it.	
	As you said, take one step at a time. Now replace the highlighted template with the following Smalltalk code:

```
defaultColor
   "Return the default fill style
for the receiver"
   ^Color green
```

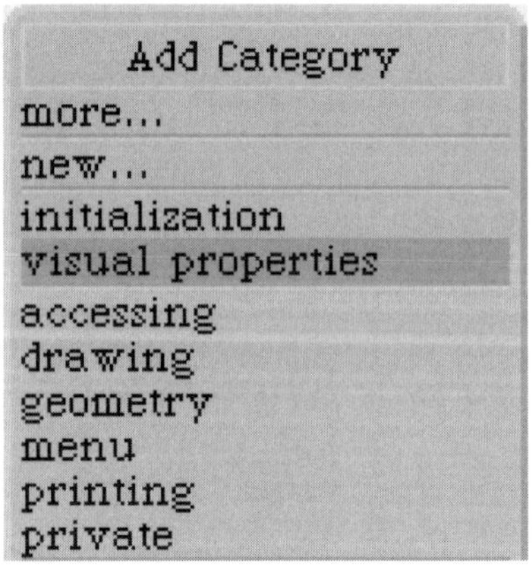

Add Category
more...
new...
initialization
visual properties
accessing
drawing
geometry
menu
printing
private

Figure 15–17
The Add Category menu

JIM	OBJECTIVE WIZARD
	After the new method has been accepted into the runtime, you can create a new instance by evaluating this expression in a Workspace:
	`GreenRectangleMorph new openInWorld.`
	A `GreenRectangleMorph` will be created and displayed in the upper left corner of the Squeak environment.
And what should I do with it?	
	You should test it and see if it behaves in the same manner as the built-in `RectangleMorph` shown in Figure 15–18.
	You have now extended a class and created a class of your own.
That was a tough one. But I followed you. Is there another morph we can work with? I think I need to get used to doing this stuff.	
	Yes, let us tackle something else. In your investigation of the `SimpleButtonMorph`, you will meet a morph that must be moved by its handle.
What do you mean? I can't just grab it like other morphs?	
	Thus far, all of the morphs that you have met from this particular section of the Morphic hierarchy, including `GreenRectangleMorph`, could be grabbed directly and moved by the cursor. This ability is no longer available. If you look at the methods in the `event handling` category in class Morph, you will see that the `handlesMouseDown: evt` is defined to return `false`. The outcome of this is that unless you override the `handlesMouseDown:` the default

Figure 15 18
A GreenRectangleMorph

JIM	OBJECTIVE WIZARD
	behavior of a `Morph` (or any of its subclasses) is such that it can be picked up and relocated on the screen by the cursor. The class `SimpleButtonMorph` is the first subclass of `Morph` in this hierarchy to redefine the method `handlesMouseDown:`.
Okay.	

	This time, when you create the Morphic object, assign the returned value to a local variable. Enter and evaluate the following Smalltalk expression in a Workspace:
	`aSimpleButton := SimpleButtonMorph`
	`new openInWorld.`
	A small morph bearing the label **Flash** will appear in the upper left corner, as shown in Figure 15–19.

Okay. But what are we doing with a morph this time?	
	If you have not surmised so yet, the purpose of our investigation in this section is to change the morph's label. A method that fulfills this exact need is already defined for the class. The method that you need can be found in the `accessing` category. The correct method is `label:`.
Great. So, I can change "Flash" to say something else?	
	Yes, in order to change the displayed label from **Flash** to **ObjectLand**, enter and evaluate the following expression in the Workspace: `aSimpleButton label: 'ObjectLand'.` The displayed `SimpleButtonMorph` now has the appearance shown in Figure 15–20.

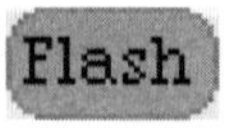

Flash

Figure 15–19 A SimpleButtonMorph with its default label

ObjectLand

Figure 15–20 A SimpleButtonMorph with a new label

JIM	OBJECTIVE WIZARD
That wasn't as tough as I expected. Maybe I'm getting the hang of all this.	
	Yes, Jim, with some guidance and practice, I think you will continue to make good progress. In fact, let us move on to an exploration of yet another morph.
	In your exploration of the `IconicButtonMorph`, you are going to complete two tasks. The first task will be to revisit the idea of embedded morphs. However, in this case, you are going to reverse the embedding process.
So, I'll un-submorph?	
	I suppose that you can look at it that way, if it suits you. You are going to disassemble a composite morph.
	The second task is to define another class of your own. This time, you are going to inherit from `IconicButtonMorph` in order to create `SmileyIconicButtonMorph`. Your new class will be designed to replace the default image of `IconicButtonMorph` with an image of the ubiquitous smileyface.
That sounds neat.	
Do we start just as we started other tasks in this chapter?	
	You will begin, as always, by instantiating a new morph—an `IconicButtonMorph`. It should look like the one in Figure 15–21.
Hey, that's cute.	

Figure 15–21
An IconicButtonMorph

JIM / OBJECTIVE WIZARD

Objective Wizard: The key to your next experiment will be learning how to identify the individual morphs that make up a composite morph.

Jim: That sounds as if it could be complicated.

Objective Wizard: This identification is actually quite easy to do, and it is based on something that you already know how to do.

Jim: That's a relief. I do much better when I'm building on stuff I already know. Still, it all feels so new to me.

Objective Wizard: I think identifying the individual morphs that make up a composite morph will feel a bit familiar, but if it does not, that is all right. Just take it step by step. You can use blue-button clicks to single out the morphs. The first click will identify the root morph, the next click will single out the first submorph of the root, and so on. You can examine this process by experimenting on the `IconicButtonMorph` that you just instantiated. When you have identified the submorph in your composite morph, it will look like the image in Figure 15–22.

Jim: Is there a halo for each submorph?

Objective Wizard: Good question. You should note that the Morphic halo is available for each and every morph in a composite morph. This means that the techniques that you have learned for

Figure 15–22
A SketchMorph submorph

JIM	OBJECTIVE WIZARD
	manipulating and investigating morphs are available for the individual morphs. With this in mind, you probably will want to open a separate Inspector on each of the two morphs that comprise the `IconicButtonMorph`.
Okay, I remember Inspectors. Now, what about the disassembling you talked about?	
	Now, you are going to disassemble the morph. Once you have identified the `SketchMorph`, you can use its black handle to move it to a new location. Observe, via the Inspectors, that the owner of the `SketchMorph` is no longer the `IconicButtonMorph`. In fact, during the period in which the `SketchMorph` is being moved by its handle (as demonstrated in Figure 15–23), its owner is the cursor—a `HandMorph`.
Ah, my favorite complex morph so far.	
	You should take note of the values of all of the `owner` and `submorph` instance variables.
So, now it's in parts?	
	Sort of. You have completed the disassembling. The second part of this section is concerned with the creation of a new user-defined class.
A smiley-face class?	
	Yes. The new class, `SmileyIconicButton`, replaces the default Squeak image of the `IconicButtonMorph` class with a new image.

Figure 15–23
Two disassembled Morphs

JIM | OBJECTIVE WIZARD

In the class `SmileyIconicButton`, the default image is created in the method `setDefaultLabel`. This method makes use of another method defined in the `IconicButtonMorph` class—`labelGraphic:`. The `labelGraphic:` method takes `aForm` as a parameter. In order to supplant the default image with the smiley-face image, you must instantiate a new `Form`. This `Form` will be the argument in the message.

The class comment for `Form` describes it as "A rectangular array of pixels, used for holding images."

What does that mean?

The class `Form` can be used to handle a variety of image types: gifs, jpegs, and bitmaps. For your task, a new `Form` can be instantiated by the following Smalltalk code. Be mindful of the fact that this Smalltalk code expects to find an image named `'smiley1.gif'` in the same directory as your Squeak virtual machine. This image, and several more that you will use in a later project, is available on your book's CD.

```
Form fromFileNamed: 'smiley1.gif'
```

So, your task in this section is to create a subclass of `IconicButtonMorph` that overrides the `setDefaultLabel` method. In doing so, your redefined method must send the `labelGraphic:` message to itself, with an argument that is `aForm`. The `Form` will display a smiley-face image.

So, I need some code now?

The Smalltalk code necessary to define the class is shown below:

```
IconicButton subclass: #SmileyIconicButton
instanceVariableNames: ''
classVariableNames: ''
poolDictionaries: ''
category: 'ObjectLand'
```

JIM | OBJECTIVE WIZARD

The code for the redefined `setDefaultLabel` method is as follows:

```
setDefaultLabel
      self labelGraphic:
         (Form fromFileNamed: 'smiley1.gif')
```

Hold your horses, now. Let me catch up. I have to make sure I type this code correctly.

Okay, Jim, take your time. After entering and accepting the code above, you will be able to create a new `SmileyIconicButton` object by evaluating the following expression in a Workspace:

```
aSmileyIcon := SmileyIconicButton new
      openInWorld.
```

Your new morph should look like the one displayed in Figure 15–24.

Wow, that's really cute.

We are not finished yet. Finally, in this last section, you are going to use inheritance to extend `SmileyIconicButton`. The new class will differ from its superclass in that, when the button is clicked, it plays a short animation.

Like a cartoon?

It will not be too fancy, but, yes, we are going to animate the smiley face. I think you'll like what you see. Taking a cue from its behavior, the name of this class is `AnimatedSmileyIconicButton`.

Figure 15–24
A SmileyIconicButton Morph

JIM | OBJECTIVE WIZARD

Before you begin, there are two topics that were mentioned earlier that need to be touched on again: event handling and animation.

Jim: Okay, it sounds familiar, but what do I need to know about event handling?

In event handling, there are two separate parts to a mouse click: down and up. In your case, you are going to handle the up event. Naturally enough, the Smalltalk method that handles this event is named `mouseUp:`. The `mouseUp:` method takes a single `MorphicEvent` object, `evt`, as an argument.

Jim: Okay. And what about animation? That's an OO thinking style, right?

Well, yes, but here we mean it literally, rather than as a thinking process. Animation is about moving images. The Morphic framework has built-in methods that coordinate this task. Among the Morphic methods that you will be using are: `step`, `stepTime`, `startStepping`, and `stopStepping`.

The key task for this class is to display a sequence of images after receiving the `mouseUp:evt` message. The resulting animation is of a smiley face that opens its eyes, sticks out its tongue, and then waggles its tongue.

Jim: That sounds so great!

You should start with the class definition. Your definition should reflect the fact that the new class will inherit from `SmileyIconicButton`. A first pass at the definition is shown below.

```
SmileyIconicButton subclass: #AnimatedSmiley
        IconicButton
   instanceVariableNames: ''
   classVariableNames: ''
   poolDictionaries: ''
   category: 'ObjectLand'
```

JIM	OBJECTIVE WIZARD
Okay, I'm typing, I'm typing.	
	Next, you should think about the behavior of this class. As mentioned above, the primary task of this class is to display images. As you saw in the `SmileyIconicButton` class, the images will be instances of the `Form` class.
I remember. How many forms will I be using to show the smiley face doing all these things?	
	In this case, you will be working with seven instances of the `Form` class. The seven `Form` objects represent the seven different images that it will take to produce the required animation. The ordering of the images is important.
So, the ordering creates what happens when?	
	Yes. The first image is already the default, or start-up, image.
The basic smiley face?	
	Yes. You need to order the rest of the images so that the first image of the animation is actually the second overall image.
What do you mean?	
	Well, the initial image is where you begin. It is a resting image, so to speak. It is where you want to end as well. So, it is not really part of the animation sequence—not part of, shall we say, the movement we are crudely making.
Okay, I think I understand.	
	Good. You want the animation to finish in such a way that the button appears as it did before you clicked it. In other words, the last image of the animation needs to be the first overall image.
Right, the beginning and the end are the same image.	
	The images will be stored in an instance variable. The preceding description of the animation suggests that the instance

JIM | OBJECTIVE WIZARD

variable will be responsible for a fixed number of ordered images. In light of this, it seems that the appropriate collection class for the job is the `Array`. A good name for the instance variable is `imageArray`. You will also need an `Integer` instance variable to use as an index into the array. You should name this variable `index`.

Go ahead and add the two instance variables to your class definition.

What should that look like?

Now, it should look like this:

```
SmileyIconicButton subclass:
     #AnimatedSmileyIconicButton
   instanceVariableNames: 'imageArray index'
   classVariableNames: ''
   poolDictionaries: ''
   category: 'ObjectLand'
```

The methods of this class have a variety of tasks to perform. The instance variables need to be initialized.

How do I initialize?

This task will require an `initialize` method. In order to retrieve the Form objects that are stored in `imageArray`, you will need to provide an accessor method for that instance variable. Also, you will need a method that can be used to update the displayed image.

Whew, lead the way.

The Morphic framework animation methods that you will need to override are `stepTime` and `step`. The `stepTime` method controls how often the `step` message is sent—that is, controls the speed at which the animation executes.

So, `step` signals an image change, and `stepTime` con-

JIM	OBJECTIVE WIZARD
trols how quickly the changes occur?	
	Good. The frequency of the message sends is given in milliseconds. In this class, the `step` method will be responsible for requesting that the images be displayed. It will also decide when it is the appropriate time to stop the animation. You will also make use of the `startStepping` and `stopStepping` methods. The `startStepping` method initiates the sending of `step` messages. The `stopStepping` method ends that activity.
So, we are able to set up a defined sequence? We control the beginning and the end?	
	Yes. Finally, you will override the `mouseUp:` to handle the event by starting the animation. When you are adding methods, it is a good habit to categorize the methods as you add them.
What do you mean?	
	The methods that you will add and their appropriate categories are listed in Table 15–1.

Table 15–1 Methods and their categories

Method Name	Category Name
`Intialize`	`initialization`
`mouseUp:`	`event handling`
`imageArray`	`accessing`
`updateImage`	`accessing`
`step`	`stepping and presenter`
`stepTime`	`stepping and presenter`

JIM | OBJECTIVE WIZARD

All of the methods for AnimatedSmileyIconicButton are presented in the following listing.

```
initialize
      super initialize.
   count := 0.
   imageArray := Array new: 7.
      ImageArray at: 1 put: (Form fromFileNamed: 'smiley2.gif');
         at: 2 put: (Form fromFileNamed: 'smiley3.gif');
         at: 3 put: (Form fromFileNamed: 'smiley4.gif');
         at: 4 put: (Form fromFileNamed: 'smiley5.gif');
         at: 5 put: (Form fromFileNamed: 'smiley4.gif');
         at: 6 put: (Form fromFileNamed: 'smiley6.gif');
         at: 7 put: (Form fromFileNamed: 'smiley1.gif').

mouseUp: evt
   super mouseUp: evt.
   count := 0.
   self startStepping.

imageArray
   ^imageArray.

updateImage: aCount
   | aForm |
   aForm := self imageArray at: aCount.
   self labelGraphic: aForm.

step
   count := count + 1.
   count <= imageArray size
            ifTrue: [ self updateImage: count ]
            ifFalse: [ self stopStepping ].

stepTime
   ^250
```

I'm typing as fast as I can. Am I ready to see the animation yet?

After you have entered and accepted each of the methods, you should create an instance of AnimatedSmiley IconicButton. Click on it and watch the animation.

Jim	Objective Wizard
Wow, this animation is so neat! I'm not sure I understand what I've done, but I think I get most of it.	
	Yes, Jim, I think you are catching on. Just be patient, and practicc. You should also take some time to experiment with this animation in the same way that you have experimented with other morphs.
I'm off to experiment right now. Thank you, Wiz.	
	You are welcome, Jim. Bon voyage.

Summary

New Terms

Inspector	Forms
`RectangleMorph`	`GreenRectangleMorph`
`SimpleButtonMorph`	`IconicButtonMorph`
`SmileyIconicButton`	`AnimatedSmileyIconicButton`

What Did You Learn?

- How to change the state (that is, color, submorphs) of a `Morph` object.
- How to use an Inspector.
- How to use inheritance to create a new Morphic class.
- What `SimpleButtonMorph` and `IconicButtonMorph` are.
- How to create a simple animation using the Morphic framework.

Words of Wisdom

Morphic is a powerful and flexible user interface. To use it effectively, you must understand its built-in event-handling and animation capabilities. Further investigation of the classes that make up the Morphic hierarchy will show you how to build your own Morphic applications.

To Do List

Trace the inheritance hierarcy of the `MovingEyeMorph`. Could you change the default color of the pupil? The iris? Do it.

Pick a game from the `Morphic-Games` category—FreeCell, Tetris, and so on. Analyze the Smalltalk code for the entire game. Take it apart to see how it was put together. Think of a game that you might like to create for yourself (Tic-Tac-Toe, anyone?). Write that game.

Glossary

ACTIVATE. *See* METHOD ACTIVATION.

ANALOGY. A thinking tool that is useful in object-oriented thinking and design. Refers to the comparison of an understood framework to one that is less well understood in the hope of transferring knowledge about the first to the second. *See also* OBJECT-ORIENTED THINKING and METAPHOR.

ANIMATION. A thinking tool that is useful in object-oriented thinking and design. Refers to the imaginary visualization of an object's behavior. Visualizing the behavior often brings out hidden complexities. *See also* OBJECT-ORIENTED THINKING and VISUALIZATION.

ANSWER. *See* RETURN.

ANTHROPOMORPHISM. A thinking tool that is useful in object-oriented thinking and design. Refers to the assignment of human personality characteristics to virtual objects. Some common personality types are managers, teammates, and rovers. *See also* OBJECT-ORIENTED THINKING.

APPLICATION. A solution to some problem expressed in Smalltalk (or some other programming system). It generally consists of one or more windows that provide a user interface and some objects that represent the information and behavior of the RealWorld objects in the solution. *See also* ITERATIVE DESIGN AND DEVELOPMENT, WINDOW, and METHODOLOGY.

ARGUMENT. An object passed to a method as part of a message send. Binary and keyword messages always have arguments; unary messages never do. Blocks can also be passed arguments.

ASSIGNMENT. Refers to the operation that changes the object that a variable references. This operation is done using the colon-equal (:=) operator and is *not* a binary message send. *See also* VARIABLE.

BINARY MESSAGE. A message that has exactly one argument. Binary messages consist of one or two special characters. Binary messages are normally used for messages that do arithmetic or that compare two objects. *See also* MESSAGE and ORDER OF EXECUTION.

BLACKY. A large, black, four-footed entity that exists in the RealWorld. Although he looks like a dog, Blacky's IQ is estimated to be 402. We have no explanation for this, but our current hypothesis has to do with time travel, advanced five-dimensional processing systems, and superconducting drool. *See also* GARBAGE COLLECTOR.

BLOCK. A piece of code packaged as an object. Blocks are implemented as instances of `Context` or one of its subclasses. A block is defined by surrounding a piece of code with brackets (`[]`). Blocks can have zero, one, or two arguments.

CLASS. A template for creating objects. All objects are instances of a class; classes define the behavior for their instances and what instance variables they will have, but not the values of the instance variables. *See also* CLASS VARIABLE, INSTANCE, and INHERITANCE.

CLASS VARIABLE. A variable associated with a class. The variable is accessible by the class's methods and instances. It is also accessible to the class's subclasses and their instances. Class variables always start with capital letters. *See also* VARIABLE, POOL VARIABLE, and INSTANCE VARIABLE.

COMPUTERLAND. The normal Von Neumann-style computer. Also used to refer to systems that are created (programmed) in a procedural fashion, since the procedural paradigm is close to the hardware.

DO IT. A menu option that compiles and executes selected code in a text pane. Also refers to the action of selecting a piece of code and executing it with this menu option. *See also* SHOW IT.

DYNAMIC BINDING. Capability of some object-oriented systems to choose the code that will be executed when a particular message is sent at runtime. Also called *late binding. See also* POLYMORPHISM, MESSAGE, and METHOD.

ENCAPSULATION. Objects have a private inside, which consists of variables and methods, and a public outside, which consists of a message interface. You can access an object only by sending it a message. This protection and containment of variables and methods is called *encapsulation. See also* MESSAGE and MESSAGE INTERFACE.

EXPRESSION. See STATEMENT.

GARBAGE COLLECTOR. Refers to the part of the Smalltalk runtime system that looks for unused objects and reclaims the memory they are using. Creating (and understanding) garbage collectors is an arcane art that is best left to those brilliant and slightly insane people who enjoy such things. All we need to know is that garbage collectors keep us from having to worry about deallocating objects that we are done with. Blacky is sometimes referred to as the garbage collector, for several unsanitary reasons. *See also* BLACKY.

IMPLEMENTORS. The methods that implement a particular message as in "the implementors of the `at:put:` message." Also used to refer to the option on the methods menu in the class hierarchy browser that creates a list of the implementors of a message. *See also* SENDERS.

INHERITANCE. When a class is given the state and behavior of its superclass, which it can then add to or modify to define the new class, this passing down is called *inheritance.* Classes inherit the following from their superclasses: instance and class methods, class variables, and instance variable templates. *See also* SUPERCLASS and SUBCLASS.

INSTANCE. An object that is not a class. It can also mean any object that has some particular class, as in "The variable `A` contains an instance of `Array`." *See also* CLASS and OBJECT.

INSTANCE VARIABLE. A variable associated with an instance. The variable is accessible by the instance methods of the instance's class and by the instance methods of its subclasses. Instance variables always start with lowercase letters. *See also* VARIABLE, POOL VARIABLE, and CLASS VARIABLE.

ITERATIVE DESIGN AND DEVELOPMENT. An approach to development of software that recognizes and takes advantage of the incomplete knowledge we have of the Problem-World. The basic idea is to make something work and then iteratively refine it until it is good enough to use. The only major problem with this approach is deciding when you're done. This approach seems to work very well for dynamic, object-oriented development environments such as Smalltalk. *See also* PROBLEMWORLD, METHODOLOGY, and SOLUTIONWORLD.

JIM. A RealWorld human who needs to learn about object-oriented stuff. This person truly exists. He lives in Milwaukee, Wisconsin and is, indeed, a software developer.

KEYWORD MESSAGE. A message that has one or more arguments. Keyword messages are made up of keywords. Each keyword begins with a letter and ends with a colon. There is one keyword for each argument. *See also* MESSAGE and ORDER OF EXECUTION.

LATE BINDING. *See* DYNAMIC BINDING.

LOCAL VARIABLE. A variable that is available only during a single method activation. Local variables are defined within the source code for a method. These variables are sometimes called *temporary variables. See also* VARIABLE and METHOD ACTIVATION.

MESSAGE. Something that is sent to an object to invoke a behavior when that behavior is defined in a method. *See also* UNARY MESSAGE, BINARY MESSAGE, KEYWORD MESSAGE, and METHOD.

MESSAGE INTERFACE. The set of nonprivate messages to which an object responds. *See also* PRIVATE METHODS.

METAPHOR. A thinking tool that is useful in object-oriented thinking and design. Refers to a concept that is being transferred from its traditional framework to another, where it is used as an analogy or for implicit comparison. *See also* OBJECT-ORIENTED THINKING and ANALOGY.

METHOD. A piece of code that is executed when an object receives a message. *See also* MESSAGE and METHOD ACTIVATION.

METHOD ACTIVATION. When a message is sent to an object, it activates a method. This means that it creates any local variables, passes the arguments to the method's parameters, makes `self` refer to the receiver object, and then executes the method code. *See also* METHOD and MESSAGE.

METHODOLOGY. A system or method, usually including a sequential process that helps someone move from the ProblemWorld to the SolutionWorld. There is considerable commercial and research activity centered around the creation and standardization of a design and/or development methodology for object-oriented systems. So far, everything available has holes big enough to chuck a horse through, but things are getting better.

MORPH. A graphical object. The name is from the Greek for "shape" or "form." A morph has a visual representation that can be manipulated via its halo and handles.

MORPHIC. One of the two user interfaces that Squeak supports. Morphic is a framework for constructing interactive graphical applications. The Morphic interface was originally developed for the Self programming language.

OBJECT. What this whole thing is about. It is used as a focus for creating computer applications and can be used in a similar fashion in design and general thinking. An object is assumed to have two things: some information it keeps on its "inside" and some behavior or actions that can be activated from its "outside."

OBJECT-ORIENTED DESIGN. A prolonged object-oriented thinking activity applied to a specific problem and solution. The process may be assisted by the use of a methodology. *See also* OBJECT-ORIENTED THINKING and METHODOLOGY.

OBJECT-ORIENTED PROGRAMMING. Programming using objects and messages. It doesn't really work unless you are using a programming language designed with constructs supporting objects and messages. It can also mean the use of the concepts of class, inheritance, encapsulation, and polymorphism.

OBJECT-ORIENTED THINKING. Thinking about a problem or solution in terms of objects and messages. It can also include the use of the concepts of class, inheritance, and polymorphism. *See also* OBJECT-ORIENTED DESIGN.

OBJECTIVE LIBRARIAN. The virtual entity that serves as a repository for all information concerning the Squeak programming environment, particularly its tools and history. The Objective Librarian is helpful, friendly, and well organized.

OBJECTIVE WIZARD. A virtual entity with a great deal of knowledge about object-oriented things, particularly those connected with Smalltalk. The knowledge and personality are based on several RealWorld people. *See also* WIZ.

OBJECTLAND. A virtual reality lurking inside dynamic, object-oriented systems such as Smalltalk. It is where most of this book takes place.

OOD. Acronym for Object-Oriented Design.

OOP. Acronym for Object-Oriented Programming.

OOT. Acronym for Object-Oriented Thinking.

ORDER OF EXECUTION. The order in which messages are sent and operations are performed within a Smalltalk statement. The ordering is from first to last: code in parentheses, unary messages, binary messages, keyword messages, assignment, and return. Multiple messages of the same type evaluate from left to right. *See also* UNARY MESSAGE, BINARY MESSAGE, and KEYWORD MESSAGE.

OVERRIDING. Methods inherited from a superclass can be overridden by writing another method with the same name in the subclass. The new method will be used instead of the one from the superclass. Only methods can be overridden. *See also* `SUPER` and INHERITANCE.

PANE. A section of a window controlled by an instance of a subclass of `SubPane`. Panes are designed to interact with the user in a particular way. There is a set of classes that implement different interaction strategies such as text manipulation, list handling, and graphics. *See also* WINDOW.

PERSPECTIVE. A thinking tool that is useful in object-oriented thinking and design. Appropriate usage in this context would be "changing of perspective." Refers to the purposeful changing of the way an object is thought of or viewed. *See also* OBJECT-ORIENTED THINKING.

POLYMORPHISM. An important, but difficult to explain, capability of object oriented systems. Refers to the ability of an object to decide how it will behave when it receives a message. In other words, the same message can invoke different behavior from different objects. In Smalltalk, the behavior is defined by a method, and polymorphism is implemented using dynamic binding. In some object-oriented systems, polymorphism is built into the inheritance system, limiting its scope. In Smalltalk, however, polymorphism does not have this limitation. *See also* DYNAMIC BINDING.

POOL DICTIONARY. A collection of pool variables stored in an instance of `Dictionary` and referenced by a global variable. Pool dictionaries are generally used to store collections of related constants. For example, there is a pool dictionary called `CharacterConstants`. To use a pool dictionary, simply specify it in a class definition. The pool variables in the dictionary will then be accessible to all the class and instance methods for that class. *See also* POOL VARIABLE.

POOL VARIABLE. A variable that can be shared between classes. Pool variables are grouped into pool dictionaries, and the entire dictionary is specified in the class definition. Pool variables always begin with capital letters. You should treat pool variables in the same way as constants. Do not—I repeat, do not—try to use an assignment on them. *See also* POOL DICTIONARY.

PRIVATE METHODS. Methods that are marked as private in their comments and are intended to be sent only from other methods in the same object. Private messages, which are messages that activate private methods, are not considered to be part of an object's message interface. This is a design distinction and is not enforced by the system. *See also* `SELF` and `SUPER`.

PROBLEMWORLD. The domain of a problem that needs to be solved. *See also* SOLUTIONWORLD and REALWORLD.

PSEUDO VARIABLE. A way of referring to an object that works like a variable but is not a variable. The Smalltalk language contains five pseudo variables: `true`, `false`, `nil`, `self`, and `super`. The first three are used to access instances of the classes `True`, `False`, and `UndefinedObject`, respectively. The last two are used to reference the receiver object. *See also* `SELF` and `SUPER`.

REALWORLD. The place we live in. Sometimes called *reality* or *real life*. *See also* OBJECTLAND, COMPUTERLAND, PROBLEMWORLD, and SOLUTIONWORLD.

RECEIVER OBJECT. When a message send is being discussed, this term refers to the object that receives the message. Within a method activation, this refers to the object that receives the message that activated that method. *See also* `SELF` and METHOD ACTIVATION.

RETURN. Every message send returns an object. To control what is returned, you must use a return operation in the method code. The return character (`^`) should be placed before the statement that returns the object you wish to return from your method. A return also causes an exit from the method. This is sometimes called answering an object.

`SELF`. The pseudo variable `self` refers to the receiver object. It is most commonly used to send messages—often private messages—to the receiver object. *See also* PSEUDO VARIABLE, PRIVATE METHODS, RECEIVER OBJECT, and `SUPER`.

SENDER OBJECT. When a message send is being discussed, this term refers to the object whose method activation is sending the message. This is confusing until you realize that all executing code in Smalltalk is happening within some object. *See also* RECEIVER OBJECT and METHOD ACTIVATION.

SENDERS. The methods that send specific messages, as in "the senders of the `size` message." Also used to refer to the option on the methods menu in the System Browser that creates a list of the senders of a message. *See also* IMPLEMENTORS.

SHOW IT. A menu option that compiles, executes, and displays the returned object from selected code in a text pane. Also refers to the action of selecting a piece of code and executing it with this menu option. *See also* DO IT.

SOLUTIONWORLD. The domain of the solution to a problem. There is often a large overlap between the ProblemWorld and the SolutionWorld. *See also* PROBLEMWORLD and REALWORLD.

STATEMENT. A chunk of Smalltalk code consisting of zero or more message sends and terminated by a period. Also called an *expression.*

SUBCLASS. Denotes an inheritance relationship between two classes, as in "`Array` is a subclass of `Collection`." A subclass inherits from its superclass. *See also* SUPERCLASS and INHERITANCE.

`SUPER`. The pseudo variable `super` refers to the receiver object, but it behaves differently when it is sent a message. Messages sent to `super` start their search for the associated method in the objects superclass. `super` is used only to access methods that have been overridden. *See also* `SELF` and SUPERCLASS.

SUPERCLASS. Denotes an inheritance relationship between two classes, as in "`Number` is the superclass of `Integer`." A subclass inherits from its superclass. *See also* SUBCLASS and INHERITANCE.

TEMPORARY VARIABLE. *See* LOCAL VARIABLE.

UNARY MESSAGE. A message that does not have any arguments. Unary messages always begin with lowercase letters. *See also* MESSAGE and ORDER OF EXECUTION.

VARIABLE. A sequence of characters, beginning with a letter, which, when used in source code, refers to some object. It is called a variable because it does not have to refer to any particular object, just to some object. You can change the object that a variable references by using an assignment statement. Variables come in several flavors, which differ in where they can be used. *See also* ASSIGNMENT, INSTANCE VARIABLE, CLASS VARIABLE, and LOCAL VARIABLE.

VISUALIZATION. A thinking tool that is useful in object-oriented thinking and design. Refers to the imaginary conceptualization of an object's attributes or state. Often combined with the animation of the object's behavior. *See also* OBJECT-ORIENTED THINKING and ANIMATION.

WINDOW. A construct that exists on a computer screen. It generally contains one or more subparts called panes. This "screen thing" is used to do some particular task such as writing words, editing method code, doing arithmetic, and so on. *See also* PANE.

WIZ. Nickname for the Objective Wizard, used only by those who know him well.

WORKSPACE. A window in the Smalltalk programming environment, which is used to type in brief pieces of temporary code. It is often used for testing, trying out some simple code, or keeping track of various odds and ends. It is a very simple and useful programming tool. *See also* WINDOW and APPLICATION.

For More Information

The Objective Librarian recommends the following resources from the ObjectLand library. The information in these resources was uncovered during many tours to ObjectLand and can help to lead you in the direction you are seeking.

General Sources of Information

OOPSLA Conference Proceedings

ECOOPS Conference Proceedings

Journal of Object Oriented Programming (JOOP)

For Further Reading

Alpert, S.R., Brown, K., and Woolf, B. 1998. *The Design Patterns Smalltalk Companion.* Reading, MA: Addison-Wesley.

Beck, K. 1997. *Smalltalk Best Practice Patterns.* Upper Saddle River, NJ: Prentice Hall PTR.

Budd, T.A. 1991. *A Little Smalltalk.* Reading, MA: Addison-Wesley.

Budd, T.A. 1997. *An Introduction to Object-Oriented Programming.* 2nd ed. Reading, MA: Addison-Wesley.

Burnett, M., Goldberg, A., and Lewis, T., eds. 1995. *Visual Object-Oriented Programming: Concepts and Environments.* Greenwich, CT: Manning.

Cox, B. 1991. *Object Oriented Programming: An Evolutionary Approach.* Reading, MA: Addison-Wesley.

Goldberg, A. and Robson, D. 1989. *Smalltalk-80: The Language and Its Implementation.* Reading, MA: Addison-Wesley.

Guzdial, M. 2001. *Squeak: Object-Oriented Design with Multimedia Applications.* Upper Saddle River, NJ: Prentice Hall PTR.

Guzdial, M. and Rose, K. 2002. *Squeak: Open Personal Computing and Multimedia.* Upper Saddle River, NJ: Prentice Hall PTR.

Ingalls, D. 1980. *The Smalltalk-80 System Design and Implementation.* Palo Alto, CA: Xerox, Palo Alto Research Center.

Ingalls, D. 1983. "The Evolution of the Smalltalk Virtual Machine." In *Smalltalk-80: Bits of History, Words of Advice*, Glen Krasner, ed. Reading, MA: Addison-Wesley.

Kaehler, T. and Patterson, D. 1986. *A Taste of Smalltalk.* New York: W.W. Norton.

Lambert, K.A. and Osborne, M. 1997. *Smalltalk in Brief: Introduction to Object-Oriented Software Development.* Boston, MA: PWS.

Liu, C. 2000. *Smalltalk, Objects, and Design.* New York: toExcel.

Pinson, J. L. and Wiener, R.S. 1988. *An Introduction to Object Oriented Programming and Smalltalk.* New York: Addison-Wesley.

Skublic, S., Klimas, E.J., and Thomas, D.A. 1996. *Smalltalk with Style.* Upper Saddle River, NJ: Prentice Hall PTR.

Taylor, D. 1992. *Object-Oriented Information Systems: Planning & Implementation.* New York: Wiley.

Taylor, D. 1998. *Object-Oriented Technology: A Manager's Guide.* 2nd ed. Reading, MA: Addison-Wesley.

Index

Page numbers followed by *f* and *t* indicate figures and tables, respectively.

N

CD-ROM Warranty

Addison-Wesley warrants the enclosed disc to be free of defects in materials and faulty workmanship under normal use for a period of ninety days after purchase. If a defect is discovered in the disc during this warranty period, a replacement disc can be obtained at no charge by sending the defective disc, postage prepaid, with proof of purchase to:

Editorial Department
Addison-Wesley Professional
Pearson Technology Group
75 Arlington Street, Suite 300
Boston, MA 02116
Email: AWPro@awl.com

Addison-Wesley makes no warranty or representation, either expressed or implied, with respect to this software, its quality, performance, merchantability, or fitness for a particular purpose. In no event will Addison-Wesley, its distributors, or dealers be liable for direct, indirect, special, incidental, or consequential damages arising out of the use or inability to use the software. The exclusion of implied warranties is not permitted in some states. Therefore, the above exclusion may not apply to you. This warranty provides you with specific legal rights. There may be other rights that you may have that vary from state to state. The contents of this CD-ROM are intended for personal use only.

More information and updates are available at: http://www.awl.com/cseng/titles/0-201-73114-2